Our Time

Our Time

Finding Hope in a Climate Crisis

Alasdair Skelton

BLOOMSBURY ACADEMIC
NEW YORK • LONDON • OXFORD • NEW DELHI • SYDNEY

BLOOMSBURY ACADEMIC
Bloomsbury Publishing Inc, 1359 Broadway, New York, NY 10018, USA
Bloomsbury Publishing Plc, 50 Bedford Square, London, WC1B 3DP, UK
Bloomsbury Publishing Ireland, 29 Earlsfort Terrace, Dublin 2, D02 AY28, Ireland

BLOOMSBURY, BLOOMSBURY ACADEMIC and the Diana logo are trademarks of Bloomsbury Publishing Plc

First published in the United States of America 2026

Copyright © Alasdair Skelton, 2026

Cover design: Diana Nuhn
Cover image: Emmy Skelton Kockum

All rights reserved. No part of this publication may be: i) reproduced or transmitted in any form, electronic or mechanical, including photocopying, recording or by means of any information storage or retrieval system without prior permission in writing from the publishers; or ii) used or reproduced in any way for the training, development or operation of artificial intelligence (AI) technologies, including generative AI technologies. The rights holders expressly reserve this publication from the text and data mining exception as per Article 4(3) of the Digital Single Market Directive (EU) 2019/790.

Bloomsbury Publishing Inc does not have any control over, or responsibility for, any third-party websites referred to or in this book. All internet addresses given in this book were correct at the time of going to press. The author and publisher regret any inconvenience caused if addresses have changed or sites have ceased to exist, but can accept no responsibility for any such changes.

Library of Congress Cataloging-in-Publication Data
Names: Skelton, Alasdair, author.
Title: Our time : finding hope in a climate crisis / Alasdair Skelton.
Description: New York : Bloomsbury Academic, 2026. | Includes bibliographical references and index.
Identifiers: LCCN 2025023828 (print) | LCCN 2025023829 (ebook) | ISBN 9798765163467 (hardback) | ISBN 9798765163474 ebook | ISBN 9798765163481 epdf
Subjects: LCSH: Global environmental change—History | Climate change adaptation | Climate change mitigation
Classification: LCC GE149 .S59 2026 (print) | LCC GE149 (ebook)
LC record available at https://lccn.loc.gov/2025023828
LC ebook record available at https://lccn.loc.gov/2025023829

ISBN: HB: 979-8-7651-6346-7
ePDF: 979-8-7651-6348-1
eBook: 979-8-7651-6347-4

Typeset by Deanta Global Publishing Services, Chennai, India
Printed and bound in the United States of America

For product safety related questions contact productsafety@bloomsbury.com.

To find out more about our authors and books visit www.bloomsbury.com and sign up for our newsletters.

For the children in Parliament Square.
This book is based on a true story.

Contents

Acknowledgments ix
Prologue x

1 Boxing Day 1
2 Time 7
3 Climate 17
4 Stromatolites 21
5 Granite 33
6 Snowball Earth 41
7 The Hyperthermal 51
8 The Ice Age 59
9 Queen Kristina 67
10 The Last Dance 75
11 2020 83
12 Climate Live 91
13 Heat Waves 97
14 Floods and Droughts 103
15 Melting Ice and Rising Seas 111
16 Niko 121
17 Sophia 127
18 Conference of the Parties 133
19 Alternative Futures 143

20 Our Story 149
21 The Oak Tree 167

Notes 175
Index 195
About the Author 200

Acknowledgments

I wish to take this opportunity to thank my mother for teaching me the art of storytelling, my family in Sweden for their encouragement, my friends whose loved ones were taken from them by the tsunami for sharing their sorrow, and the children in Parliament Square for opening my eyes to the climate crisis.

Prologue

Four Million Years

It is as if I had lived for four million years.
It is as if I had been born when the mighty Eridanos River flowed down from northern Sápmi and across the open grasslands, which once stretched from Sweden to Finland in the place that would become the Baltic Sea.

It is as if I had walked my first steps alongside the pine-clad shores of that magnificent river, captivated by the beauty of its sparkling waters, while far from where I walked, the ancient land of Beringia that once bridged from Alaska to Siberia was flooded over, separating the old world from the new.

It is as if I had spent my childhood years, playing in the soft northern sunlight, with the sweet scent of pine all around me, while on the other side of the ocean, the Isthmus of Panama rose out of the sea, making two Americas into one.

It is as if I had come of age as the Gulf Stream was born in the shelter of that isthmus, and I had witnessed its warm and moist air masses sweeping across Scandinavia for the very first time, only to stage a battle that it would not win with the frigid air masses of the far North.

Prologue

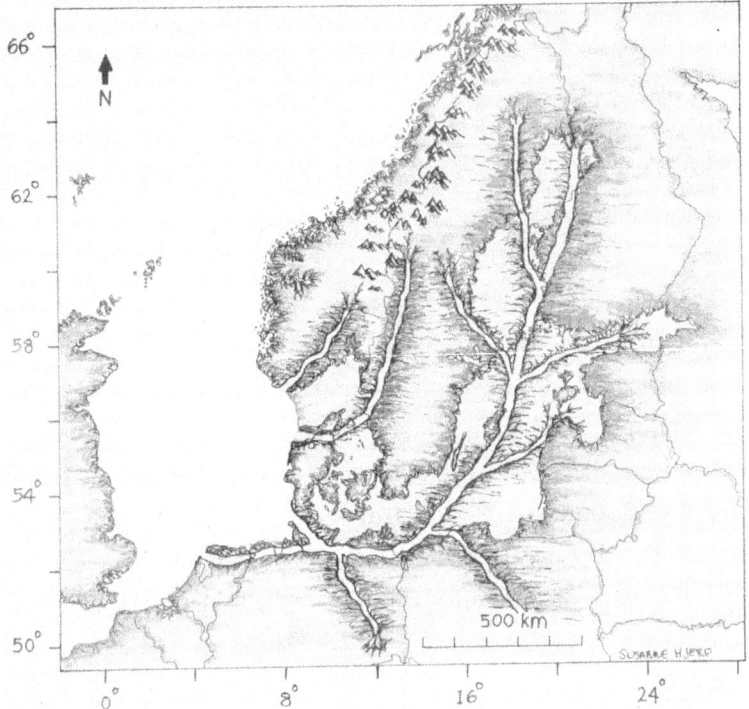

Figure 0.1 *The Eridanos River, between Sweden and Finland, four million years ago. Artwork: Susanne Hjerp*

And then I would have seen the first snowflakes fall.

And my most productive years would have been overshadowed by the vast ice sheets that advanced and retreated across the northern landscape, remolding it, time and time again.

And I would have started to write this story as the most recent of those ice sheets retreated and unveiled the place that I call home.

And in this moment that we will spend together, we could stand on the plains of India and watch the Himalaya rising before us at such speed that we could see them growing taller by the day. Or if we were to sail from Southampton to New York City on a mighty ocean liner, we could watch Iceland emerging from beneath the waves as we passed it by. And as we began approaching our final destination, we would find that the continents were moving so fast that if we paused for just a few minutes, we would see North America drifting away. We could watch as, one by one, the pinnacles of Manhattan set beneath the western horizon.

It is all happening so fast.

Too fast.

The Earth has warmed by more than a degree since I was born.[1] The same geological machinery that submerged the Valley of Eridanos, that tore open the Bering Straits, that built the Isthmus of Panama, that powers the rise of the Himalaya, that makes Iceland emerge from the sea, and that drives North America away from Europe also controls the climate.[2] That elegant machinery would have taken four million years to achieve the warming that we have experienced since I was born in 1968.[3]

It is the speed at which the climate crisis is unfolding that terrifies geologists.

Over four million years, living things can adapt to a degree of warming. Over fifty years, they cannot.[4] The steady rise of carbon dioxide in the air that we breathe tells us that the chemistry of the Earth is being turned inside out. This places unimaginable strain on the delicately interwoven geological systems upon which life depends. It is why some geologists now speak about a sixth mass extinction.[5]

I am one of those geologists.

Even so, I find it hard to feel the immediacy of the climate crisis. It seems so faraway. It is as if it were happening somewhere else or in some far and distant future. But it is not. It is here. It is now. It is racing toward us. The planet that we live on is warming faster now than at any other time we know about in the past four billion years.

The climate crisis is like a wave as it approaches the shore. It is rising in front of us, bearing down upon us, and it will shatter into pieces all that we hold dear. Yet we find it so hard to feel it coming. But we must. We must try.

Sometimes metaphors can help us. They can be easier to relate to than a truth we find so abstract that it does not feel real. I will begin this story by sharing one with you. It has helped me. I hope that it will help you too.

I do not want to scare you. But I must. Because we must face the climate crisis: not only in our minds, but also in our hearts. We must feel its immediacy. Then we must turn and run as if our lives depend on it, because they do.

This is how we create hope. This is how we create real hope of a future that is both possible and beautiful, not only for ourselves, but also for our children, and for the 8.7 million species of plants and animals[6] with which we share our cherished home.

The metaphor I will share with you is based on a true story.

It begins with a man standing on a beach, and it takes place on Boxing Day.

1

Boxing Day

The man standing on the beach is in his thirties. He holds a child in one arm and a handheld video camera in the other. He is filming the sea. The Sun has crested the line of jungle-covered hills behind him. It is gaining strength. There is a gentle offshore breeze. It has enough strength to make the palm crowns rustle, but no more. The sky is a perfect blue.

The sea seems very faraway. In the foreground, mounds of reddish-brown sand are heaped up on the landward side of a group of granite skerries. There is a wooden fishing boat on one of these mounds. It is lying on its side. The skerries are completely bare of vegetation. Between a few of the skerries are pools of seawater. In one of them, a tourist floats on an air mattress. There is a local boy there. He is collecting fish from the pool and putting them in a carrier bag.

The sea behind the skerries is calm, barely agitated by the breeze. Two military vessels, one larger than the other, glide effortlessly southwards, cutting parallel wakes behind them. There is also a small fishing boat. It does not seem to be moving. Further out to sea, there is a dark ridge running parallel with the shore. I guess it is made of sand or gravel. It is too faraway to be sure. Beyond this ridge, a line of waves is breaking.

There are a few other people on the beach. Most are tourists. But there is also a small group of locals. They are standing together watching the sea. One of them shouts something. An older man. I do not know what he said, but the boy collecting fish stops and turns.

It is 10:27 a.m. on Boxing Day.

There is a second line of waves behind the first one. Both lines must be moving landwards because the dark ridge is now gone. The military vessels continue drifting southwards. The fishing boat turns slightly.

A tourist alongside the man with the video camera walks toward him. He is holding a beach towel. He shakes it, climbs up from the beach onto the grassy path that leads toward the resort, and walks away.

There are other shouts, and the group of locals start walking up from the beach. First slowly. Then their pace quickens. The boy who was collecting fish drops his bag and starts to run. He is trying to catch up with them. He is far behind.

Another man, a tourist from Sweden, is standing near the wooden fishing boat. He is tall and quite handsome. His face is rugged from working out-of-doors. His hair is blonde and slightly wavy. His eyes are blue. He turns to watch as the locals walk up from the beach. There is a woman beside him. His wife. I can only see her from behind. There are three girls. His children. They are blonde like their father. The oldest girl is in her teens, and the youngest is maybe five or six years old. The middle child is standing furthest away. She is watching the sea. They were playing, but now they are standing still. Absolutely still.

The first line of waves reaches the military vessels. It engulfs them. For a split second, neither vessel can be seen. But then both emerge again, one after the other, behind the line of waves. The fishing boat faces the waves head-on. It rises. It stands on end. Then it flips, and it is gone. Then the second line of waves comes.

The man who was filming the sea lets go of his camera. He turns and starts to run. He holds the child tightly. The camera dangles freely, held by a strap across his shoulder.

The video camera is still on. The footage it captures as the man runs with the child contains flickering glimpses of footpaths, roads, buildings, and then jungle. Hurried footsteps. Panting. Sixty seconds after the man escapes from the beach, a resounding crash drowns the sounds of running.

This is when the wave hit the shore.

It is 10:30 a.m. on Boxing Day.

The crash fades away, replaced by steady thuds. The man is still running. The child is silent, or too quiet to be heard. It takes several minutes before the man stops and turns. His breathing is heavy. The flickering of jungle foliage is replaced by a sweeping panorama of destruction. The village of Khao Lak in southeastern Thailand is gone. Its beach. Its holiday resorts. Its people. The sea has engulfed it all in raging swathes of turbid gray.

Then chaos becomes ordered. The entire bay is filled with one massive whirlpool. It rotates clockwise. It will continue until the bay empties and the land emerges once again. But we do not see this happen because the video comes to an end.

Official reports state that more than four thousand people were killed by the Indian Ocean tsunami in Khao Lak on December 26 (Boxing Day), 2004.[1] Over five hundred of them were from Sweden.[2] The man who was standing near the wooden fishing boat was not one of them. He survived. His wife survived. So did his eldest and youngest child. But his middle child did not. He came home without her.

How could it happen? The safety of high land was only a few minutes away. Why did he stand and watch his children playing as a tsunami wave swept in to strike them down? Why did he not grab onto them and run?

The reason is obvious and painful: He did not know it was a tsunami. No one did. Nobody who was standing on that shore knew that the faint line on a seemingly distant horizon was the deadliest tsunami in human history.

They couldn't have.

There are three reasons why.

One. The Earth is curved. If you are standing on a beach right down by the sea and are of average height, what you perceive as the horizon is only four and a half kilometers away. No one standing on that beach would have seen the tsunami at all until it crested the horizon. This happened nine minutes before it hit the shore.[3]

Two. A tsunami wave grows taller as it approaches the shore. It would have been less than half of its full height when it crested the horizon. Standing on that beach, it would have been hard to see. It would have been more or less impossible to tell it apart from a normal wave.

Three. There is no sense of scale. Not until the military vessels were engulfed and the fishing boat was flipped would a person standing on the beach have had any way of knowing how large the wave that was approaching them actually was. The fishing boat was flipped sixty seconds before the tsunami reached the shore.

Then all it took was a moment of hesitation, and there was no longer enough time to escape.

I am a geologist. I do research on tsunamis. Yet, I am certain that if I had been there, I would not have known either. I too would have stood and watched until it was too late.

But there were signs.

There had been a low rumbling sound two and a half hours earlier. It was no louder than a passing truck, but it was detected by seismologists all around the world. The low rumbling was caused by seismic waves from a faraway earthquake. Its magnitude was 9.1.[4] It was the largest earthquake on Earth in more than forty years. It triggered the tsunami.

The sea had pulled back from the shore, exposing the granite skerries and stranding the fish that the local boy was collecting from the pool on which the tourist was floating on an air mattress. It was not low tide. It was the tsunami. When we envisage a wave rolling in from the sea, we think of its crest rising upward. We seldom think of its trough sinking downward. But at Khao Lak, the trough of the tsunami arrived before its crest. This is why the sea receded.

And then there was that faint line on the horizon. Seemingly small and faraway, until it engulfed the military vessels and flipped the fishing boat over.

There were signs.

And there are signs.[5]

There are heatwaves, each one hotter than the one before. There are droughts, each one longer than the one before. There are floods, each one more powerful than the one before. Wildfires are happening more often, and each one is more destructive than the one before.

The ice is melting and the sea is rising.

It is all happening faster and faster.

The climate crisis is rising from behind the horizon. It is like a tsunami wave.

And as it rises and bears down upon us, we stand, and watch with our children playing around us.

We are watching, but we are not seeing.

The signs are there, but we find ourselves unable to read them.

In a few moments the fishing boat will be flipped over, and we will understand the power of the wave. Moments later, it will hit the shore.

But we do not feel it coming. We do not feel its immediacy.

There is high ground behind us. There is still time. But we do not run. Instead, we stand still with our loved ones beside us, and we watch as the climate crisis engulfs us all.

This is now.

This is our time.

It is time to run.

Figure 1.1 *Memorial to a loved one who was taken by the tsunami wave in Khao Lak on December 26, 2004.*

2

Time

There is a moment before and a moment after a tsunami strikes. Those moments are different beyond comprehension. One moment is still and peaceful. The other is chaos. All that separates those moments is time. The place is the same, but the time is different.

The place you are now, wherever it is, has been perilously hot, and freezing cold. It has been a safe haven for living things, and it has been hostile and barren. It is part of a story that is as old as the Earth and its story will continue in a future that is as long again. We are here for a moment in that story. There is a time before us, and there is a time after us. Both times are vast beyond our wildest dreams.

As adults, we have lost the ability to comprehend time. But this is an ability we once had. The vastness of time was real for us when we were children and before the age of fantasy abandoned us in favor of the rationality of adulthood. When fantasy was still real for us, we could listen to stories about wondrous creatures which walked the Earth many millions of years ago, and those stories became real for us. We were a part of them. We were there. We could walk with dinosaurs in our minds and really be there with them. The concept of a million years had real physical meaning.

But as we became older, we lost this gift. We are still able to speak knowledgeably about millions of years, but the words lack meaning. They lack feeling. Yet, for us to be able to see the climate crisis in its true enormity, we need to find this meaning again. We need to feel it. This is not easy, but we can try. One way is to use a metaphor for time. This is a representation of time at a scale we find easier to comprehend. I will share one with you now.

It begins with the Moon.

I ask you to picture yourself standing out-of-doors in a place where it is still dark enough to see the stars. You watch as the Moon rises and the stars around it fade away, overpowered by its brightness. But you are not really seeing the Moon at all. Instead, you are seeing what the Moon looked like one second ago. This is because it took one second for sunlight reflected by its barren stony surface to reach wherever you are standing. The reason for this is that the Moon is so faraway.

I ask you now to return in your mind to the same place on a fine morning and picture yourself watching the Sun as it rises above the horizon. But you cannot do this because you are not really seeing the Sun at all. You are seeing what the Sun looked like eight minutes ago. The Sun is so faraway that it takes eight minutes for its own light to cross all the space between it and the place where you are standing. This is true even though sunlight crosses space at the breathtaking speed of three hundred thousand kilometers every second. The Sun is that faraway.

Now I ask you to reflect for a moment on what you were doing eight minutes ago. Whatever this was is what an observer, positioned as faraway as the Sun is, would see you doing right now.

Moving further away, we come to Alpha Centauri. This is our nearest cluster of stars. It looks like a single star and appears as the brightest one in the constellation Centaurus, which belongs to the southern sky. When we look at it, aided by a telescope, we do not see what it looks like today. Instead, we see what it's nearest star looked like four years ago.

What was the world like four years ago? This is the world an observer, positioned as faraway as the nearest star of Alpha Centauri, would see right now. How much has changed since then?

Looking further afield, we come to the Andromeda Galaxy. This is not our nearest galaxy. The smaller Magellanic Clouds are nearer. But the Andromeda Galaxy is more beautiful, at least I think so. When we look at this galaxy, we do not see what it looks like right now. We see what it looked like 2.6 million years ago. This is when the Arctic Ocean froze over for the first time and the Ice Age began. This is the chapter of Earth's history we live in now. It is a chapter during which ice sheets advance and retreat from the poles to a rhythm set by our planet's dance around Sun. At our moment in this dance, the ice sheets have retreated, revealing the beautiful, and vibrant world, with its multiple shades of green, that we are now a part of.

And last of all, with the mighty power of the Hubble space telescope and what astronomers call "a ripple in spacetime," we can glimpse a distant star called Earandel. When we look at this massive star, we are seeing what it looked like 12.9 billion years ago.[1] This is less than one billion years after the Big Bang which is when it might all have started, we think. And then, with the knowledge that the normal lifespan of a star the size of our Sun is around ten billion years, and aware that larger stars have far shorter lifespans, we are left wondering if the star we are now looking at, Earandel, is still there.

If we now turn around and race forward through space and time for eight billion years, we will reach the moment, four and a half billion years ago,[2] when the Earth and the solar system which it belongs to emerged from a swirling cloud of gas and dust.

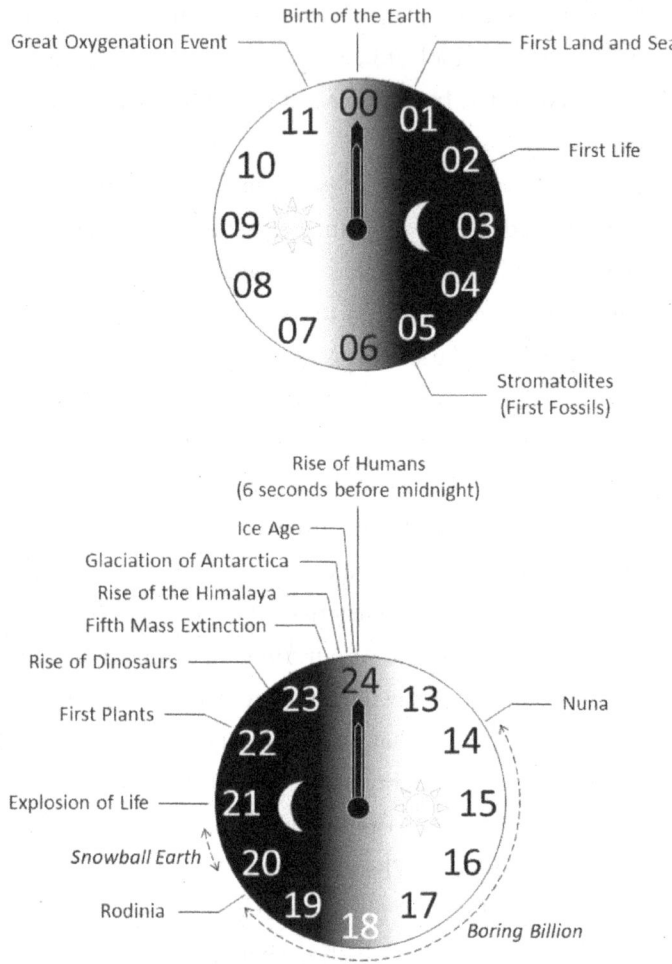

Figure 2.1 *Geological time represented by twenty-four hours.*

This is the point at which our analogue for time begins.

We will represent Earth's four and a half billion years of history, from its moment of formation until the moment you are reading this sentence, with a period of twenty-four hours, beginning at midnight on the first day and ending at midnight at the start of the second day.

At midnight on the first day, Earth was an unpleasant place. The air was an asphyxiating mixture of nitrogen and carbon dioxide.[3] Its surface was an ocean of glowing hot magma which was being bombarded relentlessly by meteorites from space. One of them was so large that, when it struck the Earth, a part of it was ejected back into space. That part of the Earth became the Moon[4] which you just imagined yourself looking at.

In the first hour of the morning, Earth became nicer. The chemistry of one of the oldest mineral grains ever found, a grain of a mineral called zircon that occurs naturally as beautiful golden-brown four-sided prisms, tells us that land, and sea might already have existed 4.4 billion years ago.[5] We also learn that a complex set of chemical reactions between the land, the sea, and the air had been set in motion in a manner that stabilized Earth's climate,[6] not only back then, but also from that point forward until the present day.

In the second hour, we suspect that life emerged. We suspect this because, encapsulated within zircon grains which were formed at that time, we find small pieces of a second mineral, a mineral called graphite,[7] a mineral that is made of pure carbon, a mineral that occurs naturally in sheets that are so thin that we cannot see them as separate from one another. By carefully analyzing these miniscule pieces of graphite, we find that the carbon atoms that they are made of weigh considerably less than normal carbon atoms. Because we know that living things prefer to build themselves of lighter carbon atoms rather than heavier ones, we suspect that these pieces of graphite were once living things.

Even if we suspect that life emerged in the second hour of our geological day, the oldest fossils that are recognizable as fossils were not formed until the morning. These are stromatolites. They are shaped as domes or pillars, ranging in size from centimeters to meters. The oldest ones (we have found so far) were built by colonies of blue-green algae three and a half billion years ago.[8] Blue-green algae are not algae at all. They are a type of bacteria called cyanobacteria. These are single-celled organisms which capture energy from the Sun by the life-giving process biologists call photosynthesis.

Today, photosynthesis generates oxygen as a by-product. In the beginning, it did not. The by-products of cyanobacteria making their own cell membranes by photosynthesis were sulfur and water. It was not until mid-morning of our geological day that photosynthesis became "oxygenic," meaning that oxygen (rather than sulfur and water) was generated.

The first whiffs of oxygen that were generated by photosynthesizing cyanobacteria were consumed by oxygen-loving gases, which were emitted by volcanoes. But with the passage of time, so much oxygen was being generated that the oxygen-loving gases could take no more, and oxygen flooded the atmosphere. This was the Great Oxygenation Event.[9] It was a turning point in the story of the Earth. It was crucial for us. If it had not happened, we would not have emerged 2.4 billion years later on.

While oxygen was being poured out into the air, making it breathable for a plethora of future organisms, the surface of the Earth was being transformed. Back then, continents were far smaller, and there were many more of them than there are today. Also, continental drift was much faster, partly because continents were smaller and partly because the Earth's internal heat engine, which is what drives continental drift, was hotter back then. I ask you to envisage hundreds of fast-moving miniature continents racing around the globe, colliding, and merging with one another. This is the early Earth. With time, many small continents became fewer larger ones, until there was only one. There was one single landmass that straddled the equator. This may have been the first supercontinent.[10] It was called Nuna.

And then everything stopped. For one billion years, nothing happened, and we don't know why. Geologists call it the Boring Billion.[11] Nuna stood still. The climate stayed the same. Life carried on but did not evolve. This billion-year chapter of global nothingness continued until the evening of our geological day. Then, out of nowhere, catastrophe struck.

A "perfect storm" of geological coincidences, one of which was a rearrangement of Nuna to from a new supercontinent called Rodinia, caused the chemical reactions that had stabilized the climate for three billion years to run wild. The result was Snowball Earth.[12] Rodinia and the worldwide ocean that surrounded it froze over entirely and remained frozen for nearly sixty million years. Then came an unexplained respite which lasted for a few million years before the surface of the Earth froze over once more and remained frozen for another ten million years.

Of the many unanswered questions about Snowball Earth, one of the most fascinating is how life survived. We must ask this question because we find stromatolites from before and after Snowball Earth. Did the cyanobacteria that made them adapt to the extreme cold? Did they find warmth around volcanic vents? Or did they die out entirely and emerge again for a second time after Snowball Earth ended? We may never know for certain. But what we do know is that Snowball Earth was followed by the Explosion of Life.[13] Perhaps we would be correct if we were to envisage Snowball Earth as a biological "reboot": a point at which life was switched off and on again. And when it was switched on again, or restarted, everything was different. From a handful of single-celled organisms, which had monopolized the Earth for more than three billion years, came a cornucopia of not only single-celled but also multicellular organisms. These are the wondrous sea creatures whose fossils we collect and place on our mantelpieces. They emerged in an evolutionary explosion which lasted for millions of years. There were beetle-like creatures called trilobites that crawled on the seafloor. There were glamorous floating creatures with conical and spiral shells called belemnites and ammonites that filtered plankton from shallow warm seas. There were sea urchins. And there were multicolored corals that formed reefs for other sea creatures to live in. And there were many more.

As competition for places to live in the sea became ever harder, one or two opportunistic creatures ventured onto the land, and with them came the emergence of plants[14] and the surface of the Earth became green. From plants came peat, and from peat came coal. And with less than two hours of our geological day remaining, the coal that would power the Industrial Revolution started to accumulate far underground.

The more opportunistic land-goers grew larger and diversified. And, while the supercontinent Rodinia fragmented into pieces only to converge again to form another supercontinent, called Pangea, one group of opportunists evolved into dinosaurs and ruled the Earth for more than 160 million years.

Then an asteroid struck the Earth and killed them all.[15]

This was Earth's fifth mass extinction. It happened sixty-six million years ago with only twenty minutes of our geological day remaining. At this point in time, the Earth was in a greenhouse state. This means that the climate was extremely warm. It would have been so warm that it would not have snowed anywhere on Earth, not even at the poles. The Earth's average temperature would have been double what it is today. This greenhouse world was punctuated by curious "warming spikes" called hyperthermals.[16] These are short-lived episodes when an already overheated Earth became even hotter for reasons that we do not fully understand.

The greenhouse world ended when India escaped from Pangea as it too started breaking into pieces. India fled across an ocean that no longer exists and collided with Asia. This massive collision formed the Himalaya, a mighty range of mountains which rose up from the plains between the places where Kathmandu and Ulaanbaatar would be built fifty million years later.

The rise of the Himalaya caused the chemical reactions which stabilized climate to run wild again, but not as wild as in the run-up to Snowball Earth. Nevertheless, the emergence of the Himalaya brought about fifty million years of global cooling.[17]

When half of this time had passed and only ten minutes of our geological day remained, glaciers, and then ice sheets formed in Antarctica. The refrigerating effect of all of this ice cooled the Earth some more[18] and, with only one minute remaining, we witness the Arctic Ocean freezing over too, and the Ice Age beginning, or we would if we were to look back at the Earth from a spaceship which was somewhere amid the Andromeda Galaxy.

Long after all of this had happened, at six seconds to midnight, *Homo sapiens* emerged in Africa.[19] Our emergence was so recent that we would not even need to leave our own galaxy to look back at it happening from space.

We evolved quickly.

At seven milliseconds to midnight, five hundred million of us lived on six of Earth's seven continents.[20] We had become so many that the surface of the Earth could no longer supply us with the food we needed to feed ourselves. We solved this with chemistry. Early on, we used a mineral called gypsum to make the soils more fertile so that we could feed more of us. Later on, gypsum was superseded by phosphorus, which we extracted from the roots of ancient mountains. Then came nitrogen, which we pulled out of the air that we breathe. And so, we revolutionized agriculture, making it possible for our population to carry on growing. And it did.

Our numbers continued rising, and our species spread to all corners of the world. Some places were cold, which meant that we needed to burn ever larger amounts of wood to keep ourselves warm. And when we had cut down all of the trees, we dug peat and burned it too. And as wood and peat fell into short supply, we had no other choice but to search underground to find something to burn to keep ourselves warm. And we found it.

We found a rock called coal. It seemed too good to be true. Not only, could we burn it to keep ourselves warm, but we could burn it to power steam engines so that we could travel around the world, and we could burn it to power machines so that we could produce more for less. We could revolutionize industry.

And we found more coal. Lots more. The coal that we found had accumulated underground since the first plants had evolved on the Earth, making its surface green. We dug it up from underground, burned it, and dug up some more. And then we found oil and gas. And every time we burned coal, oil, or gas, we added carbon dioxide to the air that we breathe. And at the beginning of the final millisecond of our geological day, we had added so much carbon dioxide to the air that we had changed the climate.[21]

3

Climate

Climate is a word we hear frequently. It is often paired with "change" or "crisis" or "emergency." But what is it that we are changing? What is it that is in crisis? What is it that is in a state of emergency? What is climate?

The word climate was originally a geographical term. Long before we changed the climate, the Greek philosopher Aristotle divided the known world into five zones called climes (κλίμα).[1] There were two "frigid" climes, corresponding to the polar regions, and an uninhabitable "torrid" clime corresponding to the equatorial region. Between them were two temperate climes, which were neither too hot nor too cold. These two climes, which constituted the habitable world, were further divided by the astronomer Ptolemy into seven latitudinal zones that were also called climes. He defined them mathematically, based on the length of the longest day, such that it increased in half-hour steps from thirteen to sixteen hours.[2] This forgotten definition of climate is worth reflecting on because it reminds us that climate defines the bounds of habitability. Climate defines the limits of life.

It was not until the seventeenth century that the word climate started to be associated with weather conditions. In this presently accepted meaning, climate is defined as the average of weather, expressed

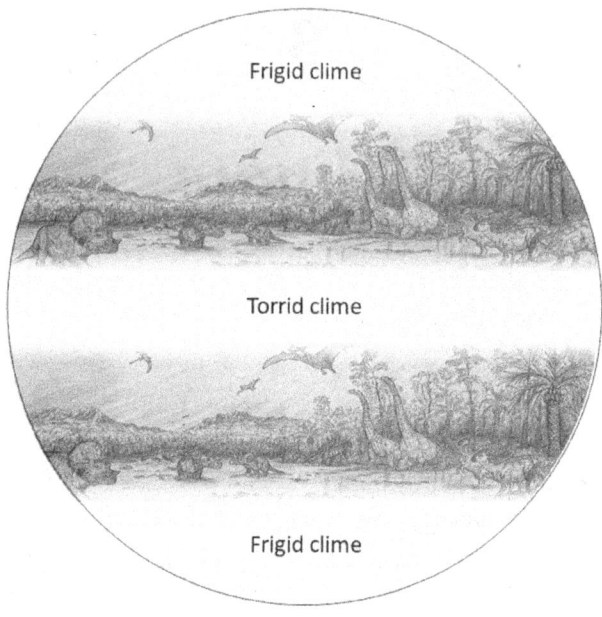

Figure 3.1 *Aristotle's five climes. Artwork: Susanne Hjerp*

by factors such as temperature and rainfall, in a certain place over a "certain period of time." According to the World Meteorological Organization,³ this certain period of time is thirty years.

I find this meteorological definition of climate concerning. This is because it is anthropocentric. It centers on humans. We can relate to a time frame of thirty years. Three decades is somewhere between a half and a third of an average human lifetime, depending on where one lives and what one's socioeconomic circumstances are. However, with this definition of climate, we lose touch with a longevity that was an implicit part of Aristotle's frigid, torrid, and temperate climes. This longevity matters. It gives us a sense of scale. Climate is big. We are small. If weather was a wave breaking on the shore, climate would be a tsunami.

As a geologist, I prefer to think of climate as a descriptor of what a part of the world is like, or what it *was* like, for the full duration of a specific chapter of geological time. These chapters are long. Geologists call them epochs, periods, eras, and eons. They range in length from thousands of years to millions of years. By thinking about climate in this way, we acknowledge its true longevity. We show it respect. And with this definition, we are forced to accept that by changing the climate, we have become geological actors.

With this in mind, I would like to reflect for a few moments on the geological meaning of climate, because to do so brings us closer to an appreciation of its beauty.

Geologists (and meteorologists) see climate as a balance of energy.[4] This energy comes from the Sun. It is radiative, meaning that it moves. It is emitted by the Sun, and eight minutes later, it is received by the Earth. Most of it is visible light. We call it sunlight. It is the difference between night and day.

Sunlight warms the surface of the Earth. If the Earth had been perfectly black (a so-called *blackbody*), its surface would absorb all of this sunlight, and its temperature would be raised from minus 270°C (which is the temperature of most of outer space[5]) to 6°C.[6] The perfectly black surface of the Earth would then radiate exactly the same amount of energy back into space, but as heat, not light. This distinction is important. A colder body radiates heat, whereas a hotter body radiates light. The Earth is colder. It radiates heat. The Sun is hotter. It radiates light.

Of course, the Earth is not a blackbody. Its surface is not perfectly black. It is full of colors. And because some of them are bright colors, one-third of the sunlight that reaches the Earth is reflected back into space. The most reflective parts of the Earth are its most brightly colored parts, such as snowfields, glaciers, and clouds. This mirror-like behavior is called the *albedo effect*. Its cooling effect would be a lowering of the temperature at the Earth's surface from 6°C to minus 18°C[7] were it not for the fact that the Earth's atmosphere has a built-in safety mechanism that stops it freezing over.

This safety mechanism is called the *greenhouse effect*. It is almost spiritual in its beauty. Its fine tuning ensures a stable climate and has done so for almost all of the past four billion years. What happens is that certain gases in the atmosphere capture the heat that radiates from the Earth's surface, and radiate some of that heat back again. These gases are called greenhouse gases. The main ones are water vapor and carbon dioxide. They work like a blanket wrapped around the Earth, warming its surface. Before we started changing the climate, the greenhouse effect warmed the Earth's surface from minus 18°C to an average close to 14°C.[8] This is neither too hot nor too cold. It is just right. The greenhouse effect warms the Earth's surface *and* by just the right amount. What I mean is that the greenhouse effect not only stops the Earth freezing over. It also stops the Earth overheating. The latter is because the greenhouse effect has a built-in "off switch."

It is important that we understand how this "off-switch" works because, by adding greenhouse gases to the atmosphere at a speed unrivaled in all of geological history, we are overriding it. In this last millisecond of our geological day, our species, *Homo sapiens*, has pushed its planetary home to a precipice, beyond which lies a freefall of perilous overheating.

To explain how this "off-switch" works, I will tell two stories. The first one is about stromatolites and the second one is about a rock called granite.

4

Stromatolites

The species *Homo sapiens* belongs to the genus *Homo* of the family *Hominidea*. This family belongs to the order *Primates* of the class *Mammalia*. This class belongs to the phylum *Chordata* of the kingdom *Animalia*. Animalia are *Eukaryotes*, which are one of the three domains of life on Earth. The other two domains are *Archaea* and *Bacteria*. They are collectively known as *prokaryotes*.

The prokaryotes beat us to it. They emerged before eukaryotes. We know with some certainty that prokaryotes have lived on Earth for 3.5 billion years.[1] Our certainty is based on finding fossils left behind by *cyanobacteria*, which are one of the prokaryotic kingdoms.

These fossils are called stromatolites. They are finely layered structures which tend to occur as mounds, domes, or pillars. They can range in size from a few centimeters to several meters across.

My favorite stromatolite is more than 2 meters across. This makes it one of the largest stromatolites in the world. It is made of an exquisite beige-colored rock and at first glance, it appears as a nearly perfect dome. However, when I look closely at its surface, I can see a honeycomb pattern in which each honeycomb cell is itself made up of closely spaced concentric rings. The honeycomb pattern tells me that this massive dome was made not by one but by hundreds of colonies of cyanobacteria. Each honeycomb cell is a single stromatolite pillar, which was made by an individual colony of cyanobacteria and the stromatolitic pillars have merged together to form the dome. The concentric rings within each of the honeycomb cells tell me that I am seeing the stromatolite pillars in cross section from above.

The colonies of cyanobacteria that made each pillar would have appeared as blue-green circular patches on the sandy bed of the sea. The seawater must have been extremely shallow, because cyanobacteria are photosynthetic, meaning that they create life by capturing energy from sunlight, and meaningful amounts of sunlight can only penetrate a few meters of seawater.

The gentle motion of waves would have agitated sand grains into suspension. These would have been carried by currents and rained down on the circular colonies, blocking out the sunlight which the tiny creatures depended on to survive. Calling on their plant-like instincts, each miniscule creature would have responded by growing upward, binding the sand grains together, and establishing itself once again on top of the sand. The cycle would have repeated, and layer by layer, solidified mounds of sand would have become domes, and domes would have become pillars, and pillars would have merged together to form the 2-meter-wide stromatolite dome I am now describing.

This wonderful creation of nature is at a place I call Stromatolite Bay. It is a sandy cove surrounded by rocky headlands atop which are grassy fields. The fields are no longer cultivated, but I can still make out parallel ridges and furrows, called lazy beds, which tell of crops having been grown in these fields in the past. On the hillside, overlooking the fields, I can see a cluster of ruined buildings. These were the homes of the families who worked this land before they were evicted to make space for the agricultural revolution.

Figure 4.1 *Close-up view of stromatolites in a sample of rock from the northern shore of Islay, Scotland.*

Behind the ruined buildings is wilderness. Stromatolite Bay is on the uninhabited northern shore of Islay. This is the southernmost island of the Scottish Hebrides. The exquisite windswept green island with its endless ever-changing skies is sometimes called the Queen of the Hebrides. The name is apt. Islay is beautiful. And it has a special place in my heart, because it is on this island that I began my training as a scientist. It was my first field area.

My first field season on Islay was in 1989. It was one year after the World Meteorological Organization and the United Nations Environment Program established the Intergovernmental Panel on Climate Change (the IPCC)[2] and tasked it with reviewing the state of knowledge about climate change, a task which would bring about the IPCC's first assessment report, a report that would give climate scientists a voice that would reach policymakers. At that time, I was unaware that this bridge was being built between science and policy. I was unaware that it mattered.

After three days of torrential rain, which I had spent trudging after my overly cheerful supervisors and listening to them exalt gleefully about how fortunate I was to have been granted such a wonderful field area, I abandoned the soggy mainland peninsula called Kintyre and boarded the ferry for the two and a half-hour crossing to Islay, leaving the gray featureless rocks (which I was supposed to find exciting) behind me.

The ferry is large. It needs to be. The crossing to Islay is made treacherous not only by the weather but also by the tidal streams that flow across the sea loch that separates the island from the Scottish mainland. The first part of the crossing was rough, which was unsurprising given the persistence of the storm that had been raging, but as the ferry rounded the northern end of a small, heather-clad island called Gigha, and made its way toward the southeastern shore of Islay, a small opening in the monotonous gray blanket of clouds allowed a shaft of sunlight to pass through, and the gloomy waters which surrounded the ship were instantly transformed to sparkling shades of blue and green. And as she continued, sailing past the white-painted distilleries, each perched on the shore by its own rocky bay, and rounded the headland which shelters Port Ellen harbor from the brutality of the western seas, the clouds parted, the shafts of sunlight merged together, the Sun was set free, and so was I.

I pitched my tent behind a copse of trees on the heather-clad hillside that overlooks the octagonal harbor with its seafront row of whitewashed houses which marks the start of the "whisky mile" that one can follow to the world-famous distilleries at Laphroaig, Lagavulin, and Ardbeg. I was proud of the brand-new "A-frame" tent that would be my home for my six-week-long field season. I rolled out my sleeping bag and stashed my belongings inside the tent. I put on a waterproof jacket, although it was no longer needed, and I put my field notebook and a few colored pencils in one of its pockets. Then, I walked down to the headland, which sheltered the harbor. It was beautiful. Before me were rocky coves, sandy beaches, and the vastness of the Hebridean sky. Around me was the pungent scent of peat smoke and malting barley that fills the nose of the finest of whiskies. As I walked toward the headland, I realized that I had no idea what I was actually looking for. The enthusiastic words of my supervisors had passed over me, and I was now well and truly on my own. I was clueless. It was the first day of my training as a scientist. I had been thrown in the deep end. I needed to figure it out for myself. The problem was that I did not know what to figure out.

Although I neither knew nor appreciated it at the time, I was unwittingly learning one of the fundamental principles of scientific inquiry. Science is not about finding answers to questions. It is about finding questions to answer.

The headland that sheltered the harbor was not one headland at all. It was several parallel headlands, each one jutting out a little further than the one before into the sea loch which separates Islay from the Scottish mainland. Each headland was covered with heather, and each of the valleys which separated them was pleasantly grassy. There was a makeshift wooden bench at the end of the grassy valley alongside the second headland. I sat down and looked at the rock which the headland was made of. It was the right thing to do. The rock looked gray to me at first, but as I continued to look at it, I began to see colors and textures. And then I took out my field notebook and started to sketch what I was looking at. This forced me to look more closely. Patterns emerged from the grayness and the headland in front of me began to tell its story.

The rock that the headland is made of is volcanic. It was formed in the magma chamber of a volcano which was located on the floor of an ocean that no longer exists. The name of that ocean is Iapetus. It formed between fragments of the supercontinent Rodinia as they drifted apart 600 million years ago.[3] The mechanics of how this happened were first described in a paper from 1962, which was written by a naval officer and geologist called Harry Hess. He called it his essay of geopoetry.[4]

This essay is the most important one ever written in geology. To explore its beauty, we can begin by following Jules Verne to the center of the Earth. When we make this journey, we find that the Earth is made up of layers. The core is metallic. It is surrounded by a massive layer of rock that behaves as if it were solid and liquid at the same time. This is the mantle. It separates the core of the Earth from its rigid outer shell. This shell is made up of plates which fit together perfectly, like pieces of a jigsaw. These plates are continually moving, carrying with them continents, and oceans. Some plates are moving toward each other, and others are moving apart. Plates moving toward each other close oceans, and the continents that flanked them collide with one another forming new mountains. Plates moving apart from each other create space for new oceans to form, and on the floors of these oceans, massive fissures open, making space for the underlying mantle to rise, and as it rises, it melts, producing magma, which forces itself upward, and makes space for more magma to rise by pushing the plates apart. This is what Hess wrote about in his essay of geopoetry. He called it *seafloor spreading*.

The next part of the headland's story happened 170 million years later. The fragments of Rodinia that had been driven apart changed direction and moved toward one another again, closing the Iapetus Ocean, and colliding with one another to form a range of mountains, as mighty as the Himalayas of today. These were the Caledonian

Mountains. Their remnants are the Scottish Highlands. The volcanic rock which the headland is made of was crushed and heated in the roots of these mountains. This volcanic rock is sandwiched between limestones. They too were crushed and heated. The effect was the same as what happens when we burn limestone in a kiln to produce lime for making cement. Carbon dioxide was burned off. But in the roots of mountains, carbon dioxide is not a gas because of the pressure. It is a highly corrosive liquid, capable of eating its way through solid rock.

As I continue to sketch the headland, I began to sketch corroded pathways along which carbon dioxide had escaped 430 million years ago. And then I asked myself: Where did it go?[5]

I had found my question.

It might seem an esoteric one. But it is not. I was (unknowingly) exploring a previously unknown mechanism whereby carbon dioxide finds its way from the Earth's interior to the atmosphere, where it becomes a greenhouse gas, capable of regulating climate, and life.

I learned more from my (often failed) attempts to answer this question than at any other time in my academic career. It was also my first encounter with carbon dioxide. To me, carbon dioxide was not a colorless, odorless, seemingly harmless gas. It was an aggressively corrosive substance which ate rocks. I had seen the damage it caused with my own eyes. I had sketched it in my first field notebook.

I was not the only scientist with a distrust for carbon dioxide. While I was measuring how much carbon dioxide had escaped from the roots of ancient mountains, a team of scientists on the other side of the world was measuring how much carbon dioxide was in the present-day atmosphere.

This team of scientists made their measurements 3,397 meters above sea level on the northern flank of Mauna Loa on the island of Hawaii. The measurement campaign was started by a geochemist called Dave Keeling in 1958. Two years later, he published a paper in which he was able to show that the amount of carbon dioxide in the atmosphere changes with the seasons. There is more carbon dioxide in the atmosphere before the summer growing season starts in the northern hemisphere and less after it ends. This is because growing plants consume carbon dioxide from the atmosphere, and there is more land and therefore more plants in the northern hemisphere. This elegant finding is not what Keeling is famed for. His fame comes from a much more sinister discovery which he alluded to at the end of the same paper. Referring to the amount of carbon dioxide in the atmosphere, he wrote: "When data extend beyond one year, averages for the second year are higher than for the first year."[6]

Five years later, Keeling coauthored a second paper. It was based on six years of data collection. The conclusion was unequivocal. The amount of carbon dioxide in the atmosphere was rising.[7] This rise had nothing to do with land plants. It was a direct result of burning fossil fuels. This was shown by another scientist called Hans Suess. He was working on carbon-14 dating of trees. Suess discovered that modern trees contained less carbon-14 than was expected. This pointed to a new source of carbon dioxide to the atmosphere that was free from carbon-14. This new source was (in Suess' own words): ". . . artificial coal and oil combustion."[8]

Thirty years later, what had become known as "the Keeling curve" showed that the amount of carbon dioxide in the atmosphere had risen by 10 percent since 1958. This curve formed the scientific backbone of the first assessment report of the IPCC which was published in 1990, one year after my first field season on Islay. Its authors chose the following wording: "We are certain [that] emissions resulting from human activities are substantially increasing the atmospheric concentrations of the greenhouse gases carbon dioxide, methane, chlorofluorocarbons and nitrous oxide [and that] these increases will enhance the greenhouse effect, resulting on average in an additional warming of the Earth's surface."[9]

The keyword in this statement is "certain." It is almost unheard-of for scientists to claim certainty. We are more comfortable with words such as "probable" or "likely." Nevertheless, all thirty-four co-authors, all of whom were among the world's leading climate scientists at that time, were so sure that our emissions were causing global warming that they signed off on the word "certain."

It was 1990, and we were already certain.

I often return to Islay with my own students. I take them to the second headland at Port Ellen, and I sit on the same makeshift bench where I began my career as a scientist and tell them how carbon dioxide escaped from the roots of ancient mountains. Although some of them will remember this story, none of them will forget Stromatolite Bay.

We walk there together from the road end at Bunnahabhainn. This is where Islay's most remote distillery lies. The whitewashed buildings are on a raised shoreline, which is above a small shingle bay and below limestone cliffs. The distillery overlooks the Sound of Islay. This is a narrow sea passage separating Islay from the neighboring Isle of Jura. It is more like a river than the sea. The incoming and outgoing tides are funneled through it at speeds up to fifteen knots.

The walk to Stromatolite Bay takes two hours. The route across the moors offers spectacular views of the southern Hebrides. Looking back, we see the mighty peaks on the neighboring island of Jura. Their conical summits are capped by quartzite. The vivid whiteness of this rock's color makes it look like snow from afar. Looking ahead, we see endless islands stretching northwards and westwards, out into the Atlantic Ocean. It is beautiful beyond belief. It is no wonder that legend tells of a far island, beyond the setting Sun, called *Tír na nÓg*, Land of the Ever-Young.

The winding path that descends to Stromatolite Bay takes us past the ruined buildings and across the fields with their lazy beds, below which not one, but hundreds of stromatolites surround the sand and shingle bay. It feels like walking into the geological past. The stromatolites are preserved with such perfection that it is almost as if the colonies of cyanobacteria which built them were still alive.

As we gaze upon that bay, I watch my students as they begin to see the exquisite beige domes emerge from the gray rocks that surround them. I do not need to show them. All I need to do is to be silent. The moment of realization will come to them if I give them the time that they need.

Once we have all seen them and we are immersed in the geological past, I sit down on top of my favorite stromatolite, the one that is more than 2 meters across, and I tell them about the faint Sun paradox.[10]

The existence of stromatolites presents us with a paradox. This is because the Sun was fainter when the cyanobacteria which made them were alive.

The Sun is a yellow dwarf star. It is a little less than halfway through its ten-billion-year-long lifetime, which will probably end around five billion years from now with it becoming a red giant and engulfing the Earth. Since the Sun formed from a spinning cloud of gas and dust, it has burned ever brighter. It is 25 percent brighter now than it was when cyanobacteria built the first stromatolite. An equation which was worked out in the late nineteenth century tells us that back then, the Earth should have been 20 degrees cooler. It should have been entirely frozen over. There could be no cyanobacteria. There could be no stromatolites.

But there were.

This is the faint Sun paradox.

Resolving this paradox is more than a question of academic curiosity. It teaches us about the "off-switch" that stops the Earth overheating. The first part of its resolution is to reframe the question. Instead of asking why did stromatolites exist when the Sun was fainter, we can accept that they did because we find their fossils and ask a different question: Why did the Earth not overheat as the Sun became brighter?

The keeper of the answer to this question is a rock called granite.

5

Granite

Although granite is the most abundant rock making up the continents, granite is not common on Islay. However, one can occasionally find granite boulders on Islay's beaches. They were carried there from the mainland by glaciers. If we retrace the winding paths along which the granite boulders were carried, we will ultimately reach the great moors of Rannoch and the high plateau of the Cairngorms. This is where I introduce my students to granite. I take them to a carefully chosen place on one of many ridges which lead up to the high plateau. Like Islay, it is among my favorite places. It was the playground of my early years.

In the early 1990s, I spent almost every winter weekend skiing there. On snowy Friday evenings, I would fill my van with gear and drive (too fast) from Edinburgh (which was where I was when I was not on Islay) to the Cairngorms, fervently hoping that the snow gates would be open. I was part of a community who popularized telemark skiing in Scotland. This is not the kind of skiing that is limited to places with ski tows and chairlifts. It is like a hybrid of downhill and cross-country skiing. It was perfect for the Cairngorms. Our free-heel telemark bindings were our passage to their wildest and most beautiful parts. We would attach skins to the bases of our skis and climb to some distant summit on the high plateau, from where we could choose from any number of spectacular gullies, each of which was packed with endless masses of snow and each of which offered an unforgettable descent made up of wondrous sweeping turns. Telemark skiing was at its absolute finest in the spring. The long evenings and forgiving spring snow made for perfect skiing. Gullies, which one would go nowhere near in the winter months for fear of avalanches, were transformed to safe havens for playful descents from the plateau to the valley floor far below. One of my favorites is called Tailor's Burn. It starts a few hundred meters east of the highest summit on the plateau. It is a 600-meter descent from a winter wonderland of snow-covered block fields to a springtime paradise far below. It maintains a perfect angle for carving wide sweeping telemark turns from its upper snowclad bowl to a point far below, where the playful mountain stream that carved out the gulley bursts out from beneath the snowpack just as it reaches the valley floor. Then comes the walkout. It is long and beautiful. It follows a wide and steep-sided valley northwards, passing several mountain springs before descending among Caledonian pines to the village far below.

And after those wonderful days in the mountains, we would converge on our favorite meeting place to share stories with kindred spirits about where we had been. This meeting place was a green-painted wooden building near the village. It was owned and run by telemark skiers who covered the costs of their own skiing habit by guiding tourists to the remoter parts of the Cairngorms. In the warmth of that building with its fragrant scent of pinewood, we would tell each other about the summits we had climbed and the gullies we had conquered.

Figure 5.1 *A telemark skier on the Cairngorm Mountains, Scotland.*

The proprietor of our meeting place was an older man, whom we (unkindly) called Eeyore after the fictitious character in A. A. Milne's stories. He rarely smiled, but on the few occasions he did, it was with a quiescent radiance that haunts me to this day. Eeyore had lived in the village "for ever." He had spent his entire life exploring the Cairngorms.

Eeyore was the first person I heard speak about climate change.

He had seen it happen. He told us how he would ski across the high tops at midsummer. It was the norm, not an exception. He spoke of a glacier near one of the summits, but that glacier was now gone. The springs we so enjoyed reminded him of the summers of his own childhood. I liked listening to his stories, but I failed to grasp their importance. I did not realize that Eeyore was one of only a few human beings who already understood the full significance of the IPCC's first assessment report on climate change. I did not understand it. I did not concern myself with either the past or the future. There were sufficient amounts of snow for my needs. Then and there. Nothing else mattered.

When I reflect back on my childhood, while sitting with my students on the ridge that leads to the high plateau, I would find myself echoing Eeyore's words. Only then I would be telling my students that the winters had become like the springs of my childhood. And I knew in my heart that this meant that the winters had become like the summers that Eeyore once spoke of.

The seasons are fading away.

The fading of the seasons meant that for the second half of the spring, I could take my students to the places where I once skied and be sure that the granite which these mountains are made of would not be hidden beneath snow.

I usually took them there in April. I took them to that place on the ridge, which leads to the plateau. On either side of the ridge are breathtaking views across forests and moors which extend northwards from the foot of the mountain to the distant sea. Strewn across the snowless ridge are hundreds of small pieces of granite. This beautiful red stone is the reason why the Cairngorms were once called the Red Mountains (*Monadh Ruadh*).

I would ask my students to each take a small piece of granite from the ground and squeeze it as tightly as they could between their fingers. To their astonishment (and mine the first time I saw it happening), what had seemed to be solid granite crumbled into pieces.

The reason that the granite crumbles is that it is weathered.

Weathering of granite is a chemical reaction. It is one of the set of chemical reactions between the land, the sea, and the air which were

Figure 5.2 *Outcrops of granite on the Cairngorm Mountains, Scotland.*

set in motion in the first hour of our geological day and which have stabilized the climate ever since.

Weathering of granite is the "off switch" that stops the Earth overheating.[1]

This is how it works:

1. Carbon dioxide in the air, rainwater, and granite react with each other to make clay and carbonic acid (which is the stuff that makes fizzy drinks fizzy).
2. The carbonic acid and clay are carried by rivers to the ocean.
3. When the carbonic acid reaches the ocean, it combines with calcium (average ocean water contains 0.04 percent calcium) to make limestone.

In other words: *Weathering of granite removes carbon dioxide from the atmosphere and turns it into stone.*

This is an "off switch" for a very simple reason. Chemical reactions happen faster at higher temperatures. If the Earth starts overheating, granite weathers faster, and carbon dioxide is removed from the atmosphere faster, weakening the greenhouse effect, and the Earth cools down again.

It's that simple and that beautiful. The slow and gentle weathering or rocks is nature's way of protecting the Earth from overheating. It is nature's way of sustaining life on Earth.

And that's not all.

The limestone, which is made in the oceans, accumulates on the ocean floor, and, in accordance with Hess' essay of geopoetry, it is carried from where it comes to rest by seafloor spreading until it reaches the edges of the oceans. Here, it plunges downward along ocean trenches into what Hess described as a kind of "jaw crusher" (a subduction zone). In its eerie depths, the limestone is heated, and the carbon dioxide it contained is burned off. It then mixes with rising magma beneath volcanoes, and it is returned to the atmosphere by volcanic eruptions.

This is the geological cycle of carbon dioxide: *Carbon dioxide is added to the atmosphere by volcanic eruptions and removed from the atmosphere by the weathering of granite.*

And it happens slowly.

Put a small piece of granite (most gravel is made of granite) in a place where you can see it. Leave it there, and when you reach the end of this book, look at it again, and ask yourself how much of it has crumbled away since you placed it there.

This is the pace of the geological cycle of carbon dioxide.

And today we are adding carbon dioxide to the atmosphere so fast that the weathering of rocks cannot keep pace. We add carbon dioxide to the atmosphere 100 times faster than all of the volcanoes on Earth do all together.[2]

We are overriding the "off switch" of the safety mechanism which sustains life on Earth. This is something which almost never happens, but when it does, the effects are catastrophic. We know this from the geological past. The safety mechanism has failed in both directions. Its failure has caused the Earth to freeze over and to overheat. As we spiral toward climate breakdown, we have a lot to learn from both of those failures. I will begin with the time when the Earth froze over entirely. It was called *Snowball Earth*.

6

Snowball Earth

To tell the story of Snowball Earth, I will return briefly to Islay, because it was the first place where evidence of this catastrophe was found. In a paper written in 1871,[1] geologist James Thomson described a curious rock from the Eastern Shore of Islay. The rock consisted of boulders embedded in mud, which had been turned to stone (mudstone). The embedded boulders fascinated Thomson because they bore all the signs of having been carried there by glaciers. This would have made perfect sense were it not for the fact that the mud had been turned to stone, a process which takes millions of years. This meant that the mudstone with its embedded boulders had nothing to do with the last glaciation, because this happened only a few tens of thousands of years ago. Instead, this curious rock from the Eastern Shore of Islay spoke of a glaciation that must have happened when the rocks of eastern Islay formed, more than 600 million years ago.

The plot thickened when it was discovered that, at that time, Islay was not where it is today. If we rewind continental drift, we find that Islay was much closer to the equator back then and far too close to have been covered by glaciers in any normal Ice Age. Yet the mudstone with its embedded boulders spoke clearly of glaciers.[2]

Climate modelers tell us that if glaciers and ice sheets did get too close to the equator, a tipping point would be passed beyond which the Earth would freeze over entirely.[3] This is because ice sheets and glaciers reflect the sunlight which would have otherwise warmed the Earth's surface. As ice sheets advanced from the poles toward the equator, more, and more sunlight would be reflected back into space and the Earth would cool down, making it easier for the ice sheets to carry on advancing. There is a point-of-no-return (a tipping point) beyond which the amount of sunlight absorbed at the Earth's surface is too little to avert runaway cooling and Earth enters a snowball state. This state is called *Snowball Earth*.

The mudstone with its embedded boulders, found by Thomson on the Eastern Shore of Islay, tells the story of Snowball Earth. The same story is told, and far more clearly, on a group of small islands further North. One of them is the Holy Isle. On a fine day, one can see it when walking from Bunnahabhainn to Stromatolite Bay. I usually pointed it out for my students, but I never took them there, because the logistics are far too challenging. Indeed, I have only been there a couple of times myself.

The first time was in 2016. This was the year that the Paris Agreement[4] entered into force. This is an agreement between 197 countries to hold "the increase in the global average temperature to well below 2°C above pre-industrial levels" and to pursue efforts "to limit the temperature increase to 1.5°C above pre-industrial levels." It was underpinned by the scientific findings conveyed by the IPCC in a succession of five assessment reports. The purpose of the Paris Agreement is to avert a climate catastrophe on the scale of the one I witnessed on the Holy Isle.

The Holy Isle is a magical place. It is one of four candidate islands for Hinba. Hinba was the site of a small monastery that was favored by Saint Columba of Iona in the sixth century for his periods of contemplation. It may also have been the burial site of his mother. The exact location of Hinba is unknown, but it could be the Holy Isle.[5] I like to imagine that it is.

The Holy Isle is uninhabited. It is small. It is one and a half kilometers long and half a kilometer across. Its northwestern side is precipitous. Eighty-meter-tall cliffs plunge vertically to a wave-cut platform far below. Its southeastern side is much gentler. Narrow coves hidden behind ridges of rock form natural harbors which offer some protection from the wrath of the western sea. The monastery that may have been Columba's retreat stands in ruins occupying a grassy alcove that is perched above one of these coves.

This is where the boatman brought us onshore. I remember looking back toward the mainland as he left. There was open sea. Then low-lying ghostly islands. On one of them stood a lighthouse. Its whitewashed walls gleamed brightly in the morning Sun. Then there was the narrow sea passage which led back to the mainland harbor. The boatman would soon be there. On the far side of the passage was a larger island. There was a slate quarry at its midpoint, which was surrounded by ruined buildings, once homes of workers, and their families and now abandoned. The grayness of this forgotten place contrasted with the pristine whiteness of the lighthouse that guided the boatman home.

I scrambled up the steep path to the monastery. I was accompanied by an older man. His name was Anthony. He was in his eighties, but he moved across the uneven terrain with the sprightliness of youth. His thick hair was as white as the lighthouse walls. He was tall and gangly. He walked with a wooden staff. Not because he needed one. He used it for teaching. He too was a geologist. On this island, he was *the* geologist[6] and, on that day, he was my teacher. He had come with me to the Holy Isle so that I could witness Snowball Earth for myself.

Snowball Earth came after the Boring Billion. This time of global stillness ended with the rearrangement of pieces of the supercontinent Nuna to form the new supercontinent Rodinia. Rodinia (like Nuna) straddled the equator. It would have been entirely barren, bereft of any form of vegetation. This is because it existed hundreds of millions of years before land plants would evolve and the land would become green. The bare rocky surface of Rodinia was like a giant mirror. It reflected sunlight—sunlight that would otherwise have warmed the Earth's surface—back into space. It was perfectly positioned for this task, as far more sunlight reaches the Earth at its equator compared with anywhere else on the planet.

This cooled the Earth.

Straddling Rodinia, forced upward by collisions between pieces of what had been Nuna, an enormous range of mountains was rising from the barren plains. The growing mountains carried with them a continuous supply of fresh granite to their cloud-enshrouded summits, where it reacted with warm equatorial rain mixed with carbon dioxide and weathered away. This drew down vast amounts of carbon dioxide from the atmosphere, converting it into carbonic acid, which was carried away by rivers to the oceans and turned into stone.

This weakened the greenhouse effect and cooled the Earth some more.

Snow began to fall on Rodinia's northern and southern shores. Snow became ice. Ice became glaciers, and their pristine white surfaces reflected even more sunlight back into space.

This cooled the Earth even more.

More snow fell. Glaciers become ice caps. Ice caps merged together.

The tipping point was passed, and the Earth was plunged into a snowball state.[7]

There are over ninety places worldwide where traces of Snowball Earth can be found. The Holy Isle is but one of them. But it is a fine one.

The grassy footpath, along which we walked, passed alongside the ruined monastery with its double beehive cell and cross slabs, both made of green volcanic stones. The footpath narrowed and turned sharply southwestwards. Anthony led. I followed. The rocks we were there to see were all around us, but we hurried past them without looking. We had good reason.

The rocks are sedimentary. This means that they have been laid down in layers. One can think of each layer as if it were a page of a book on which a story is written. The story is about what the world was like when that specific layer of rock was formed. The geologist's task is to read that story from what the layers are made of.

The layers of sedimentary rock on the Holy Isle are not horizontal as they would have been when they were first laid down. The forces that made the Caledonian Mountains had tilted them so that each layer slopes steeply downward toward the mainland. This is what gives the island its wedge-like shape. This means that as we crossed the island, we were uncovering successively older layers. The oldest layer is at the lowest point on the far side of the island. This is the first page of the story which Anthony and I had come there to read. This was where we were heading.

The path followed a raised shoreline. White cobbles that had been rounded by ancient seas were nestled within a carpet of low-cropped grass. On both sides of the path were stands of bracken that were no more than a few tens of centimeters tall. Their leaves were only just starting to uncoil. It was pleasantly dry underfoot and we were met by only a gentle breeze. Glimpses of sunshine that gave bursts of warmth filtered through a mackerel sky. Before reaching the southwestern tip of the island, the footpath turned sharply northwards and faded away. With a wind that had materialized from nowhere at our backs, we continued walking. After a few hundred meters, we climbed up a rock-strewn slope and walked along a narrow passage between a pair of raised sea stacks. Beyond them, we reached a grass-covered ledge overlooking the far side of the island. The wave-cut platform unfolded below us and the lofty summit of the northwestern sea cliffs towered above us. Between them, we could see every single layer of rock; an unbroken record of a climate catastrophe that remains unparalleled in Earth's four and a half billion-year history.

Anthony started to explain what I was seeing, but I needed no explanation. The brutality of Snowball Earth was blatantly laid out before me. At the lowermost reaches of the wave-cut platform, I could see a layer of familiar beige-colored domes. I recognized them from the northern shore of Islay. They were stromatolites. These fossil remains of colonies of cyanobacteria had occupied warm shallow waters surrounding Rodinia. Between the layers of stromatolites were rusty layers, ornamented with spectacular orange-colored rosettes of a mineral called gypsum. These are fossils of desert roses, beautiful flower-like structures made of gypsum which can only form in hot and dry deserts.

There was a layer of mudstone on top of the stromatolites. It contained fist-sized chunks of stromatolites and shattered pieces of gypsum. It was similar in appearance to the glacial rocks which were first discovered on Islay in 1871. Anthony used a technical term to describe it. It allowed us to distance ourselves from the horrific scene we were looking it. We could evade the turmoil. We could separate ourselves from the fact that we were looking at crushed pieces of life ripped up by a river of ice that flooded across the world like a tsunami in slow motion and left nothing behind but death and destruction. And then I couldn't distance myself any longer. I found myself wondering if the tiny living creatures which made the stromatolites

Figure 6.1 *Tilted layers of sedimentary rock that were laid down at the time of Snowball Earth and can now be seen on the western side of the Holy Isle, Scotland.*

froze to death as temperatures plummeted or if they were still alive as the first glaciers of Snowball Earth engulfed them.

We were witnessing a global catastrophe. Perhaps it was that mystical place. Perhaps it was the darkening sky. It was as if a spell had been cast upon us. Because I was actually there. I was 700 million years back in time, standing on the shores of Rodinia watching as it happened. I could see it in Anthony's eyes. He was there too.

But this was only the beginning. Extinction takes work. On top of the mudstone layer were encrustations of desert roses. The climate was fighting back. And resting on top of them, were more stromatolites. They were smaller than before. Their shapes were distorted. Some layers were broken and thrust up on top of one another. Life was struggling to survive. Then there was a second layer of mudstone. It was thicker than the one below, but the chunks of stromatolites and pieces of gypsum which it contained were smaller and fewer. There was less to destroy. This cycle repeated a few more times until the battle was finally lost. An ominous ravine ran parallel to the shore at the top of the wave-cut platform and the foot of the cliffs. Its blackness consumed the last few flickers of sunlight. It told of a gap in time when nothing was laid down. A geologist would call it an *unconformity*. It was when the world stopped for sixty million years. It was Snowball Earth.

Snowball Earth was not the end. It could not be. The geological cycle of carbon dioxide, whereby carbon dioxide is added to the atmosphere by volcanic eruptions and removed by the weathering of granite, would not allow it. But there can be no weathering during Snowball Earth. Every single piece of granite that might otherwise have weathered was buried beneath the ice sheets that covered the Earth. However, volcanic eruptions carried on. They melted chimneys through the ice and continued to pump carbon dioxide into the atmosphere. This meant that during Snowball Earth, carbon dioxide was added to the atmosphere but not removed. Climate modelers tell us that with the passage of time, enough carbon dioxide would have been added to the atmosphere to power a greenhouse effect so extreme that it would have been capable of ending Snowball Earth. At the point of meltdown, Earth would have been wrapped in a blanket of carbon dioxide like the one which envelopes present-day Venus. The rocks on the Holy Isle testify to the accuracy of their calculations.

The first sign of meltdown was at the base of the cliff. Anthony called it the Great Breccia. This eerie rock formation reached high above our heads. It was a chaotic mixture of vast, contorted chunks of a frozen landscape that had been ripped up by cascading icefalls as rapidly warming glaciers and ice sheets collapsed.

Draped on top of the Great Breccia came unequivocal proof of meltdown. The layer was a putrid orange color. It stretched upward toward the cliff top which was, by then, enshrouded in clouds. The rain, which had started falling, did nothing to detract from the vividness of its unnatural color. The layer was completely amorphous. It was the solid remains of carbon dioxide precipitated from poisonous air.

If anything had been alive when it formed, it would have left no trace. Yet I was compelled to imagine how it might have been. There would have been vast areas of ice everywhere, melting in the blistering heat. The asphyxiating air would be condensing all around. It would have been so acidic that it would have burned skin. A barren wasteland would have been emerging from beneath the ice only to be covered again with a poisonous coating of rusty orange foam. I stood staring. I was beginning to feel what extinction actually means.

Then Anthony's mobile phone rang, and the spell was broken. I was standing once more on a grassy platform looking at layers of rocks.

Anthony hung up. It was the boatman. He was coming back for us. There was a storm coming. We needed to leave the island.

This time, I led. We followed the passageway between the sea stacks. On the other side, we were hit by the full strength of the wind. We were buffeted sideways as we scrambled diagonally down the rocky slope to where the footpath emerged. It was a short distance before it turned, and we had the wind at our backs. We hurried along the raised shoreline and arrived back at the monastery at the same time as the boat reached the shelter of the cove where we had come ashore. We scrambled quickly down to the shore and clambered onboard. The crossing was rough, but the boatman was skilled. It only took him twenty minutes to bring us to the sheltered waters between the low-lying islands.

The catastrophe I witnessed with Anthony on Hinba really happened. A tipping point was passed beyond which Earth became virtually uninhabitable for over sixty million years.

The catastrophe that the Paris Agreement was written to avert is of a different kind. The runaway cooling which ended with Snowball Earth can no longer happen. This is because since the emergence of plants, no landmass, wherever it is placed, can reflect sunlight as effectively as the barren wastelands of Rodinia did in the run-up to Snowball Earth. The greening caused by plants makes the land surface darker and darker surfaces are less reflective than lighter ones.

However, even if runaway cooling can no longer happen, the Earth can still overheat. This is why we have the Paris Agreement.

And we know that the Earth can overheat because it too has happened before and far more recently than Snowball Earth. Times when the Earth overheated are called *hyperthermals*. We know of a few of them. The one I will tell you about happened fifty-six million years ago. It is the biggest one of them all. What is worrying is that we can see clear similarities between it and what is happening to Earth's climate right now.

Almost all known geological records of hyperthermals are found in sediments at the bottom of the ocean, which makes them challenging to study. However, a few exceptions do exist where evidence of a hyperthermal are found onshore. One such place is on an island called Fur in northern Denmark.

7

The Hyperthermal

Not even the conductor on the train from Copenhagen to Aarhus had heard of Fur. But to be fair to him, it is one of more than a thousand islands which make up Denmark. It is a small one too. It is in southern Limfjord. This shallow sea separates northern Jutland from the rest of Denmark. Fur can be reached by ferry from the northern end of the Salling peninsula.

Fur is quite beautiful. A patchwork of cultivated fields and meadows slopes gently upward from its southern shores to its tree-covered crest from where its northern slopes plunge precipitously, several tens of meters down to the waters of Limfjord. Cutting into its crest are massive scars where a fine white clay has been quarried to make cat litter and bricks. The clay, which is known locally as *moler*, is called *diatomite* by geologists because it is made of millions of tiny sea creatures called diatoms. These single-celled algae with cell walls composed of pure silica occupied the seas from which Denmark would form at the time when the northern Atlantic was no more than a narrow strait between Scandinavia and Greenland.

This time is called the Eocene. It followed on from the Paleocene, a geological epoch that spanned ten million years and began with the mass extinction that ended the reign of dinosaurs. During the

Paleocene, Earth's temperature rose steadily. This warming was powered by a rise of volcanic activity associated with the breakup of the supercontinent Pangaea. At the end of the Paleocene, global temperature may have reached an average of around 28 degrees[1] (which is around double today's average).

This is when it happened. It could have been caused by a massive pulse of carbon dioxide released by supervolcanoes. It could have been a burst of methane from northern peatlands. Or it could have been sudden melting of pockets of frozen methane far beneath the seafloor. We don't really know what caused the hyperthermal, which marks the end of the Paleocene and the beginning of the Eocene. The hyperthermal is called the *Paleocene-Eocene Thermal Maximum*,[2] a name that has been (understandably) abbreviated to the *PETM*. What we do know about the PETM hyperthermal is that it was devastating. Earth's average temperature rose sharply from an already superheated baseline to around 35 degrees. It happened quickly (but not as quickly as warming is happening today). And recovery took almost two hundred thousand years. This is how long it takes for weathering of granite to return the climate to normality after a massive pulse of carbon dioxide causes it to overheat.[3]

I was accompanied by a paleontologist when I visited Fur. She studies very small creatures that once lived in the sea, not in the rocks we were about to look at on Fur, but in sediments pulled up from the ocean floor by deep-sea drilling.

We arrived on Fur in the early evening and stayed overnight at a guesthouse near the harbor on the southern tip of the island. The soft green landscape, bathed in the golden light of the setting Sun, which rose gently behind the harbor gave nothing away about the precipitous northern cliffs we would explore in the morning. But we knew they were there. We had read about them in a memoir dating back to the 1980s.[4] The memoir was an account of "a remarkable sequence of rocks exposed in the northern cliffs of Fur." The sediments that became these rocks had captured a record of the PETM hyperthermal. They were supposedly accessible and visible in the northern cliffs.

The morning was as fine as the evening before. Eager for discovery, we set out on rental bikes with the morning sunlight warming our backs. We followed a narrow road along the coast from the harbor to the only village on the island. From there, we followed one of the roads, which climbed up onto the crest of the island. Looking back as we climbed higher, we could see the car ferry making the five-minute crossing to the Salling peninsula. We continued past several open pits from which moler clay was being quarried before we descended along a dirt road to its end, which was at a low point near the western end of the northern cliffs. Here, we left our bikes, and scrambled down a steep grassy slope to the northern shore.

According to the memoir, our route from that point was eastwards along the narrow pebble beach for half a kilometer. We would then find ourselves at the foot of a cliff called Stolleklint, where we would find the PETM hyperthermal.

We did as we were told, but it was not to be. We had come no more than a few hundred meters when we could continue no further. Ahead of us, our way forward was blocked by a landslide. A massive slurry of clay and a jumbled assortment of rocks and plant debris had washed down from the cliffs burying the pebble beach at exactly the place where the PETM hyperthermal was supposed to be.

In the cliff face, which towered above the landslide, we could see dull white layers of moler clay, which, according to the memoir, were laid down after the PETM hyperthermal. This confirmed what we were afraid of. All evidence of the hypothermal was well and truly buried, and it would remain so until the gnawing of the sea had washed away all traces of the landslide in front of us. By the time that would happen, our planet might be experiencing a new hyperthermal, one of our own making.

I continued staring at the moler clay. It contained several distinctive black layers. According to the memoir, these layers were made of volcanic ash erupted from volcanoes, which would have been close by at that time. This fit nicely with the idea that the onset of the PETM hyperthermal could be blamed on carbon dioxide from supervolcanoes.

Looking the other way along the shore, beyond the place where our bikes were parked, I could see another headland. This one was larger than Stolleklint. It was called Knuddeklint. It too was made of moler clay. I stared at it for a while, and then I noticed something. I could see the exact same volcanic ash layers as were in the cliff face above the buried hyperthermal. I was sure that they were the same layers because their thicknesses were the same and they were spaced apart from one another by similar distances. This could mean only one thing. There should also be a record of the PETM hyperthermal at the foot of Knuddeklint. But if there was, why had no one described it? Why was there nothing written about it in the memoir?

The answer became clear when we reached the headland. The massive cliffs that surrounded Knuddeklint plunged straight down into the waters of Limfjord. The pebble beach, which we had followed to reach the headland, came to an end before we got there. At this point, frustration took over. We were not going to be defeated. We left our belongings on the beach and carried on, wading out into Limfjord with the vertical cliffs of moler clay towering above us. The water was cold but not unpleasantly so. As we waded, I peered upward and tried not to think about the enormous, precariously balanced rocks which were looming above us. I doubted that the helmets we were wearing would have made a lot of difference if one of them were to have fallen. None did, and as we rounded the headland, the water became shallower, and we entered a small bay. Here, we clambered up onto a shingle beach, which was hidden in a narrow cleft between towering cliffs.

Our timing was perfect. As we clambered onshore, a shaft of sunlight shone down between the cliffs illuminating first one and then the other side of the cleft.

The molar clay was no longer dull. It sparkled a vivacious white and the black volcanic ash layers glistened in the sunlight. Once again, I recognized the volcanic ash layers from Stolleklint, but here, the record of the PETM hyperthermal was not buried. Here, we could see a layer of bluish-gray mud beneath the molar clay with its layers of volcanic ash. The mud was so dark and murky that it seemed to swallow the sunlight and give back nothing at all. It was as if the hyperthermal created its own darkness.

We stood silent, pondering over what we were looking at. The paleontologist explained that the PETM hyperthermal was recognized globally as a time when life was either absent or abnormal. In the bluish-gray mud on Fur, life was entirely absent. The diatoms which gave the moler clay its vivid white color were completely absent from the mud. In other places where evidence of the hyperthermal could be seen, paleontologists had found fossils of giant snakes and shrunken horses.

The hyperthermal has an important message for us. Its message is that in the face of accelerated climate change, living things do not give up easily. Instead, plants, and animals make desperate attempts to survive. This often happens by making panicky adaptations which result in weird evolutionary things happening. This happened during the hyperthermal and it is happening again. An animal that fails to (or cannot) change its migratory pattern or its seasonal behavior in response to climate change must change itself. This can happen in different ways. Animals can become smaller or change their shapes.

Figure 7.1 *Folded layers of sedimentary rock that were laid down at the time of the Hyperthermal and can now be seen on the northern shore of Fur, Denmark.*

Ecologists call the latter shape-shifting.[5] It means that the appendages an animal can use to cool itself down become disproportionately large. This can mean longer tails, broader wings, wider beaks, or larger ears. Some of these changes have already been seen in parrots, sparrows, finches, bats, and mice. The question one must then ask is how big can an appendage become before it is unwieldy? Like medical drugs we might take for an illness, evolutionary adaptations can have side effects. And, as with medical drugs, one might reach a point beyond which the side effects outweigh the benefits. For an animal fighting to survive in a collapsing climate, this is when its numbers start to fall and the spiral toward its extinction begins.

The PETM hyperthermal left chemical signals too, even if these could not be seen by staring at a layer of mud in a cliff. It is from these signals, we can deduce that the hyperthermal was caused by a massive amount of carbon being added to the atmosphere as carbon dioxide, maybe from supervolcanoes, or as methane from peatlands or from the beneath the seafloor, or from somewhere else entirely. We just don't know.

The situation we are now facing is quite different. This time, we know exactly where the carbon is coming from. As Suess showed us,[6] careful analysis of carbon in the present-day atmosphere confirms that a growing proportion of it comes from burning fossil fuels. We can also work out that the amount of carbon we have added to the atmosphere is fast approaching that which caused the PETM hyperthermal.

Chemical signals in the rocks that were laid down after the PETM hyperthermal tell us that granite weathered faster in its aftermath.[7] They tell us that the "off-switch" was activated. And from the return of normality that followed on from the PETM hyperthermal, we know that it worked. This might reassure us, when we consider present-day global warming, were it not for the fact that this return to normality took two hundred thousand years.

The PETM hyperthermal really happened. As with Snowball Earth, a tipping point was passed and Earth's climate spiraled out of control. The consequences were panic adaptations and species extinctions. The climate recovered, but its recovery was slow.

The bottom line is that when searching for reassurance concerning ongoing global warming, we find no comfort in the geological past.

To the contrary, a common factor for all five mass extinctions that have happened since the Explosion of Life 541 million years ago is a sudden onset of very fast climate change.[8] Whether the trigger was a supervolcano erupting or a meteorite striking, climate change was the main reason for plants and animals becoming extinct.

With this warning in mind, let us fast forward to our own geological period. This period began 2.6 million years ago with the Arctic Ocean freezing over, and it may end with the sixth mass extinction.

This is the Quaternary Period. It is more commonly known as the Ice Age.

8

The Ice Age

Humans emerged in and continue to live in an Ice Age. This is not to be confused with a glaciation. Glaciations are times during an Ice Age when ice sheets advance from the poles toward the mid-latitudes. These occur with a periodicity set by rhythmic variations of Earth's orbit around the Sun and the tilt of its axis of rotation. These variations control how much sunlight Earth receives and in which seasons. Geologists call these variations Milanković cycles after the person who discovered them.[1] There are warmer periods between glaciations. These are called *interglacials*. We live in one now. Our interglacial is called the Holocene. It is one of many interglacials in the ongoing Ice Age.

An Ice Age is far more than a glaciation. It is one of Earth's four stable climate states. Snowball Earth is another one. The others are called greenhouse and icehouse states.[2] Throughout most of its history, Earth has shuttled gracefully between greenhouse and icehouse states. This happens gradually, at a pace which is set by the making and breaking up of supercontinents. A greenhouse state is characterized by the absence of ice sheets, whereas the presence of ice sheets at one or both poles characterizes an icehouse state. Unlike the graceful transitions from a greenhouse state to an icehouse state and back again, Earth can only flip into an Ice Age.³ This happens suddenly, with neither grace, nor warning. All of a sudden (geologically speaking), polar ice sheets begin advancing and retreating in a rhythm set by Milanković cycles.

The flip which brought about the ongoing Ice Age occurred after fifty million years of global cooling.⁴ This long period of cooling followed on from the greenhouse world of the Eocene, which was the backdrop of the hyperthermal we witnessed on Fur Island. Cooling started with the rise of the Himalaya which was brought about by the collision of India and Asia. These great mountains rose from the plains that would have stretched from the present-day locations of Kathmandu to Ulaanbaatar, exposing a vast supply of fresh granite (and other rocks) to the moist tropical air. The warmth of the air and plentiful supply of granite sped up weathering, and enormous quantities of carbon dioxide were removed from the air and turned into stone. This weakened the greenhouse effect and cooled the Earth, but at a more modest pace than during the runaway spiral of cooling that led to Snowball Earth.

The rise of the Himalaya might not have brought about an Ice Age were it not for the fact that, at the same time, Antarctica drifted onto the South Pole. Antarctica split away from its sister continent, Australia, and drifted poleward, and, on arrival, it became isolated from the ocean currents, which share equatorial warmth with the polar regions. The greenhouse climate, which had presided since before the PETM hyperthermal, came to an end, and Earth's climate switched from a greenhouse state to an icehouse state. Ice sheets formed in the interior of Antarctica and expanded until the entire continent was covered by ice. This strengthened the albedo effect and cooled the Earth some more.

Then, 2.6 million years ago, partly due to a weakened greenhouse effect and a strengthened albedo effect, the Arctic Ocean froze over. This strengthened the albedo effect even more, and the Ice Age began.

It is a reflection on our anthropocentric perspective that we describe our own time as one of relative climate stability. This could not be further from the truth. An Ice Age is far from a time of climate stability. To the contrary, Earth's temperature shoots up, and down between glaciations and interglacial periods. The time we refer to when we speak of relative climate stability is called the Holocene. This is no more than the most recent interglacial period of the Ice Age which we presently live in. The Holocene, with its relatively stable climate, began after the most recent glaciation came to an end. It is (geologically speaking) short, spanning only 11,700 years. This makes it easier for us to relate to, compared with other far longer geological times. However, even although the Holocene encompasses all but the earliest stages of the rise of human civilization, we would be wise to remember that it is still no more than an interglacial after the last glaciation and before the next one.

Or at least it was.

Because of global warming caused by humans, we can no longer be certain that the next glaciation will happen at all.

Before continuing, I must dispel an understandable misconception. I sometimes encounter a belief that if global warming caused by humans were to stall or even avert the next glaciation that this would be a good thing. It would not be. This belief is founded on a common misunderstanding that it is the number of degrees of warming that kills. It is not. It is the *speed* of warming that kills.[5] Global warming caused by humans is happening more than twenty times faster now than it did at the end of the last glaciation.[6] It is happening so fast that there is no time for species to adapt.

Indeed, in its first assessment report, the IPCC wrote about a "business-as-usual" scenario which would result in 4 degrees of warming by 2100.[7] This is unprecedented. We know of no other time in the geological past when warming happened so fast. The mere idea that my children could experience a 4-degree warmer world and all that it means is not just terrifying. It is (for a geologist) unfathomable.

The reason we need to be afraid is that the speed of warming has already put more than 1 million of the 8.7 million species[8] that live on the Earth at risk of extinction.[9] So, even if it might well be true that humans can stall or avert the next glaciation or even flip the planet out of the Ice Age entirely, we need to be aware that this would almost definitely be paired with a sixth mass extinction.

This horrific reality is why we must act now to stop global warming. We really could go down in geological history as a species that caused a mass extinction. Yet it is clear from our half-hearted responses to global warming that, if we really do understand what is happening to the world around us, we fail to relate to it. We find ways of distancing ourselves from a truth that is so terrifying that in the few moments that we do succeed in relating to it, we risk breaking down entirely.

I distance myself too. I think all scientists working on climate do. It is the only way we can carry on with our work objectively. But then, all of a sudden, one gets it, and for a split second one grasps what climate change really means. The first time this happened to me was when a glaciologist was showing me traces left behind by the ice sheet, which once covered my home city of Stockholm.

Stockholm is a magnificent city. It is built on islands. The pastel colors of its older buildings are in perfect harmony with the gentleness of the northern light which illuminates them. All around the city are soft green woodlands and waterways, which glisten blue in the summer and freeze over in the winter. It was once a place of mild summers and snowy winters. Now its summers are hotter, and in winter, snow seldom lies.

The traces left behind by the ice sheet, which once covered the city, are plentiful. Every rock surface has been polished smooth, sandblasted beneath the ice sheet. Strewn around the city are erratic boulders as large as houses that have been abandoned by the ice sheet as it melted away. Many of them have been blown apart by water expanding as it freezes. Also, pressurized jets of water, charged with chunks of rock and pieces of gravel, have carved out cylindrical pits called giant's cauldrons. Some are so large and deep that one is left wondering if they are passageways to other worlds like the ones C. S. Lewis writes about in the *Chronicles of Narnia*.

Indeed, the old town is built on an island which, although partly man-made, is also part of an esker. This is a ridge of sand and gravel laid down by a river that flowed beneath the ice sheet that once covered the place where the city would be built. It is possible to follow the esker northwards past the old observatory and onwards beyond the city limits to the Royal Park. Here, one finds oneself among small rounded summits made of granite which have been finely polished by the ice sheet as it advanced southward from northern Sweden. And balanced on top of one polished summit stands an erratic boulder that weighs more than 100 tons. It was carried there from afar and then abandoned by the same ice sheet.

I remember sitting on that summit, leaning against that massive erratic boulder, peering upward, beyond the swaying treetops and far up into the sky, and trying to imagine several kilometers of ice bearing down on me from such lofty heights.

Figure 8.1 *An erratic boulder that weighs more than 100 tons and is balanced on a hilltop in the Royal Park, Stockholm, Sweden.*

It was then, and only as a passing remark that the glaciologist I know told me that Earth's average temperature, when the place that would become Stockholm had only just started emerging from beneath the ice, was only 4 degrees cooler than it is today.[10] This piece of common knowledge among Swedish glaciologists was completely new to me. Surely the Earth had been far colder. A quarter of the planet had been covered by ice sheets. But it had not been colder. Four degrees is the difference between a glaciated world and the mild climate of the Holocene in which civilization flourished.

Looking back, 4 degrees separates my own world from the end of the last glaciation. And looking forward, 4 degrees separates the climate of my childhood from the climate of my children's future. And, whereas the speed of warming since the last glaciation was 1 degree every thousand years, I have experienced 1 degree of warming in 50 years, and my children risk experiencing warming that is even faster. The breathtaking speed of global warming is far faster than all but the hardiest plants and animals can adapt to. This is why the geologist in me fears a sixth mass extinction.[11]

It is also why the father in me sometimes breaks down.

How did we end up here?
What led humanity to the point that our species can be instrumental in causing the next mass extinction?

Where does the climate crisis come from? What are its roots?

I do not know the answers to these questions, but I have some ideas. These ideas come from an exchange of letters between the French philosopher René Descartes and Queen Kristina of Sweden, which began in 1647.

9

Queen Kristina

Kristina became Queen of Sweden when she was only six years old. This was after her father, Gustaf II Adolf, was killed in the Thirty Years' War. She ruled Sweden from her eighteenth birthday and for ten more years, after which she abdicated, and converted to Catholicism. Thereafter, she moved to Rome, where she spent much of her life and where she became one of only three women to be buried in Vatican City. Kristina was exceptionally learned. She read fervently in a multitude of languages and rapidly exhausted the knowledge she deemed worth having and that was available to her in the Royal Library of Stockholm. In search of more, and after reading his works, Kristina began to correspond with the philosopher René Descartes.

When I teach scientific method to my students, I usually begin with Kristina. This is for two reasons. The first is gender equality. A walk through the history of scientific ideas is hugely male-dominated. I cannot help this, because I cannot (and should not) rewrite history, but I am also aware that unraveling whose ideas were whose is far from straightforward, and a case in point is the correspondence of Queen Kristina and René Descartes. This is far from a one-way communication in which Kristina asks questions and Descartes answers. To the contrary, Kristina seeks Descartes' opinion as a complement to her own. When I read this exchange of letters, I get a strong impression of ideas being shared and developed together by two similarly brilliant minds. The second reason I begin with Kristina is place. I could have, for example, chosen the writings of Aristotle to make the illustration which I am about to make, especially given that Aristotle's works are far older. But I prefer to begin with Kristina and Descartes because their correspondence played out in Stockholm. It makes it local, which makes it easier for my students to relate to. It is a part of their own culture. It is a part of where they come from. It is their story.

The exchange of letters carried on for two years and ended with Kristina inviting Descartes to visit her in Stockholm. It was with a mixture of gratitude and apprehension, as well as a desire to serve the Queen, which Descartes embarked from Holland to undertake the perilous sea journey to Stockholm in the autumn of 1649. Before leaving, he left detailed instructions about how the money in his estate was to be distributed and about which of his papers should be burned and which saved if he died on the journey to Stockholm. I do not know why he did this, but I suspect that he was already in poor health before he began this journey.

The month-long journey was arduous, but Descartes did not die at sea. Instead, he arrived safely in Stockholm, but as its darkest time was approaching and as the sea was beginning to freeze over. His timing could not have been worse. It was a particularly cold spell during the Little Ice Age.[1] The cause of this period of cooling, which lasted for several centuries, remains poorly understood, but a tantalizing (albeit controversial) possibility is that the Little Ice Age was the first stage of the run-up to the next glaciation, which was subsequently averted by global warming caused by humans. Again, not a good thing.

Given how bitter cold it was when he arrived, it seems fair that Descartes did not write with fondness about his time in Stockholm.

Instead, he wrote of an overall sense of intellectual abandonment and a fervent longing to return home. In his own words: "During the winter men's thoughts are frozen here, like the water. I swear to you that my desire to return to my Dutch solitude grows stronger with each passing day."[2]

Descartes resided in von der Linde House. This red brick mansion, which was, at that time, newly built in Dutch renaissance style and is, to this day, famed for its spectacular seventeenth century bay window, faced the grain harbor on the southern side of what was then known as the "City between the Bridges" and which is now known as the "Old Town of Stockholm." The mansion was also the residence of the French Ambassador, who had mediated Descartes' correspondence with the Queen by transcribing her letters to him and reading his letters to her, as was customary for that time.

The parts of their correspondence that I would like to share with you are from a letter written by Descartes on February 1, 1647.[3] This letter contains responses to requests from Queen Kristina for his opinion on certain matters which concerned her. Those matters were about the nature of love and the nature of God. His replies might help us understand the roots of the climate crisis we now find ourselves in.

Descartes' definition of love called upon a dualism, meaning that there were two kinds of love. He wrote about a kind of love that is rational and another kind of love that is passion. He described the love that is rational as coming from the mind. It was the foundation of sadness, desire, and joy. He described the love that is passion as no more than a confused thought that was aroused by some motion of our nerves. It mimics rational love.

According to Descartes, only humans could experience rational love. It was one of the characteristics that made us human. It made us different from other living things. It made us special. Passion, on the other hand, could be experienced not only by humans but also by other living things. It could be felt by nature, which was, according to Descartes, an unthinking mass.

Scholars of the humanities call this separation of nature from humanity "nature-culture dualism." This separation alone might not have led to the climate crisis were it not for a built-in hierarchy, which becomes apparent from Descartes' writings about the nature of God.

Descartes wrote that we could consider God as a supreme intelligence and that we could consider our own human minds as emanations of this supreme intelligence. This is important because Descartes considered the human mind and the soul with which it was physically joined to be what makes us human. It is what distinguishes humans from nature.

According to Descartes, the entwinement of our own human minds with God's supreme intelligence is why humans are capable of rational love. It is what makes us special. It is what makes us different from other living things.

If we consider Descartes' writings about the natures of love and God, we find ourselves faced not only with a separation of humanity from nature but also with a hierarchy. We find a philosophical basis for claiming that humans are superior to nature. This hierarchical form of nature-culture dualism makes it possible for humans to see nature as a resource which was put there for the purposes of fulfilling our needs and satisfying our desires.

For many years, when I was asked about the roots of the climate crisis, I would automatically point to the burning of fossil fuels. But with time, I have come to realize that its roots go far deeper. There is a reason we continue to burn fossil fuels when we know intellectually that we are harming nature (ourselves included) when we do so. We feel entitled to. And I suspect that this sense of entitlement stems from nature-culture dualism. It stems from a way of thinking which came far earlier than and laid the foundations for the agricultural and industrial revolutions.

Descartes died in Stockholm and not because of any conspiracy (whatever you may have read). He succumbed to influenza after nursing the French Ambassador through the same illness. As a non-Lutheran he was buried in a graveyard outside the city and alongside children who had died at the orphanage which was also outside the city. His burial was on February 12, 1650. His body remained buried in that graveyard until it was moved to Sainte Geneviève du Mont Church in Paris in 1667.

At the center of that graveyard was a small wooden chapel which was dedicated to Saint Olof. This chapel is gone now. In its place one finds Adolf Fredrik Church. This Gustavian structure with its whitewashed walls, copper plate roof, and painted black cupola is built in the shape of a Greek cross. It was inaugurated in 1774.

I go there sometimes with my students to show them a monument on one side of the altar. It is of an angel revealing a globe from beneath a black veil. It is Descartes' monument. It was commissioned by Gustav III and made by Johan Tobias Sergel. I am not sure what it depicts. If the veil really is being lifted away, it might symbolize a revelation of truth. But if one looks at another way, one sees a veil being cast over the Earth and one can envisage humanity (represented by the angel) separating herself from nature (represented by the globe).

One thing I am certain of is that it was neither Descartes' purpose, nor Kristina's, to cast a shadow across the world by laying foundations for a crisis in the future. Their pursuit of knowledge about the natures of love and God was beautiful and innocent. And so are many of the reasons that brought about the agricultural and industrial revolutions.

Figure 9.1 *Monument to René Descartes made by Johan Tobias Sergel in 1781, which can now be seen in Adolf Fredrik Church, Stockholm, Sweden.*

But as the ashes of these revolutions settle and we find ourselves amid the horrific reality of climate breakdown, we must gather our courage, hold onto one another with kindness, and venture out into the unknown. And the very first step we must take is the hardest one of all. We must leave the past behind us.

I was deeply afraid of taking that step. My intellect told me that by venturing out into the unknown we still had a chance of building a better future, but I found comfort in what I knew, so I held on to the past. Yet, I knew in my heart that the dance must end and that one dance would be my last one. And when it happened, I never even realized it. I did not know it was my last dance until the music stopped playing.

10

The Last Dance

It was on a Sunday night in mid-August 2018. The Highlands of Scotland had gathered in Stirling to say farewell to the rock band Runrig after forty-five years of playing Gaelic. I had flown over from Sweden on the Friday and would fly back again on the Sunday. My family were with me, as were many of my friends from the village and from Islay. In many ways it was a gathering of the Clans.

I did not think of the footprint of that journey until much later. The four of us emitted over 2-and-a-half tons of carbon dioxide for travel alone.[1] Our emissions weighed more than the rental car we used to get from the airport to our hotel in Stirling. But I thought nothing of it. I was so glad to be one of 25,000 fans who were there to say goodbye.

The first time I heard Runrig play was on Skye. We were crammed inside a marquee in Portree, which is the largest town on the island. It was my first summer home from university. The concentration of carbon dioxide in the air outside of the marquee was 349 parts per million.[2] It was a few months before we would cross the planetary boundary for climate change[3] but I did not know our planet had boundaries. Nor did most of us back then. Yet, Earth was already half a degree warmer than it should have been.[4]

It was the first time I heard Runrig play *Dance Called America*. It is an eerie song about a real dance from Skye, which was a visual enactment of the Highland Clearances. This was a cruel chapter of Scotland's history when many tenants were evicted from their homes to make way for agricultural improvement. Some fled to the cities to find work. Others emigrated, some to America. Hence the name of the dance.[5] The "improvers" ended the established runrig system from which the Gaelic band took its name. This practice of equitable sharing of arable and grazing land was replaced with intensive sheep farming. The land became more profitable, but only for a few. For most people, it was gone forever. It was one of many stages of our separation from nature.

This was the beginning of the agricultural revolution. Before it happened, we worked with nature to produce food. We used arable land for crops and grazing land for livestock. Afterward came a roller coaster of what seemed to be improvements. We went to war with nature for short-term gain. We initiated a battle against soil chemistry for the sake of mass production and monoculture. The mineral gypsum[6] was among our first weapons, but it was superseded by phosphorus[7] and nitrogen.[8] This is a battle we continue to fight. It is a battle that we can never win.

Phosphorus mainly comes from a mineral called apatite, which is usually green in color. It is the fifth mineral of the Mohs scale of hardness, making it harder than calcite and softer than quartz. It grows naturally as elegant hexagonal-shaped columns, which reflect the hexagonal pattern in which its constituent atoms are arranged in its interior. It is classified by geologists as an accessory mineral, meaning that it tends to occur in small quantities in rocks.

To make the rocks that contain apatite requires the extreme pressure and intense heat that can only be found where plates collide with one another and mountains are born. As streams flow across newborn mountains, minute quantities of apatite dissolve in their waters. Traces of phosphorus are released, carried downstream, and used by plants to make it possible for them to capture energy from the Sun. After serving this purpose, spent phosphorus will continue downstream to the sea, where it will accumulate in sediments on the seafloor. Because of seafloor spreading, those sediments will be carried across oceans and ultimately subducted, plunging them far beneath Earth's surface into one of Hess' jaw crushers. Deep down, rising magma will entrain them and carry them to the birthplace of future mountains where, hundreds of millions of years from now, apatite will form once again. This is the phosphorus cycle. Its design is flawless. The amount of phosphorus received by plants is just right. It is exactly what is needed for them to grow. The phosphorus cycle is finely tuned to sustain life on Earth.

A fundament of the agricultural revolution was to upset this balance. We searched the mountains for natural accumulations of apatite and found them. We mined them for phosphorus. We added it to the soil, making it possible for plants to grow in places where they do not belong. We grew more food and fed more humans. We could expand our own population. Then we did the arithmetic.

The supply of phosphorus will run out.

This is why we turned to nitrogen.

In contrast to phosphorus, we can consider the supply of nitrogen to be endless. Or almost. There are four quadrillion tons of the stuff in the air. The problem is that plants can't take in nitrogen from the air because it's in its pure form. However, plants can absorb nitrogen from ammonia, which can be manufactured from pure nitrogen. This is the principle of nitrogen fertilization. But there are three catches.

The first one is that producing ammonia from nitrogen takes lots of energy, most of which comes from fossil fuels. The second one is that microbes break down ammonia fertilizers, releasing nitrous oxide, which is a greenhouse gas that is far more potent than carbon dioxide. The third one, which applies not only to nitrogen but also to phosphorous, is that rivers carry both elements to the sea, causing eutrophication, meaning that the sea becomes enriched in nutrients. This might sound good, but the most visible effect is explosive growth of algal blooms at the expense of many other species.

The agricultural revolution did not happen on its own. While the Highlands were being brutally cleared of its age-old culture and its tenants were being evicted by the improvers, forty-year-old James Watt, working in Glasgow, made a discovery that would change humanity forever. In his squalid, poorly lit workshop, surrounded by various tools, and seemingly random chunks of machinery, he found an efficient way of turning coal into motion using the power of steam. His steam engine would power the Industrial Revolution. Its design was the first move of a game we still play with time. It is our most deadly game.

The energy that comes from coal is not from our time. It is from 300-million-year-old sunlight, collected, and stored by ancient plants that now constitute coal. Stealing this energy might seem harmless. But it is not. It comes at a price, because the plants that became coal also captured carbon dioxide from the air of the ancient past, and when we burn them 300 million years later, we move carbon dioxide from the air of the ancient past to the air of the present.

From a human perspective, our burning of ancient life was slow to take effect. The first hundred years of industrialization raised the concentration of carbon dioxide in the air by only twenty parts per million from its natural baseline of 280 parts per million.[9] This apparent slowness of change did nothing to deter the nineteenth-century Swedish chemist Svante Arrhenius from noting that, back then in 1896, we were already close to adding carbon dioxide to the air faster than it was being removed by the weathering of granite.[10] This meant that we had already saturated carbon dioxide's geological cycle. It was working at full capacity. It could take no more.

Two world wars came between this time and what many argue was the end of the Holocene and the beginning of a new geological epoch that, in the words of the *New York Times* climate journalist Andrew Revkin would come to be named "for its causative element—us." The name put forward for this new, human-dominated geological epoch by Nobel laureate Paul Crutzen[11] was "the Anthropocene." Its hallmark is known as the Great Acceleration.[12] It is the exponential rise of just about everything and the exponential fall of nature.

Since 1950, global population has increased by a factor of more than three. At the same time energy consumption and global wealth have increased far faster, by factors above 5, and 10, meaning that an average human consumes more now than before. This acceleration was made possible by fossil fuels, a truth that is confirmed by a parallel rise of the concentration of carbon dioxide in the air by more than 100 parts per million.

I did not think about any of this when I was in Portree. It was only weeks after I had met the person whom I would eventually marry, committing myself to a life overseas from my childhood home. Back then, I thought nothing of making this kind of commitment because it was so easy to move around. I belonged to the generation of low-fare flights. For as little as £1, I could fly back home. I enjoyed fossil fuels. I enjoyed them a lot.

What might have made it easier for me to understand when I was in Portree was that "349 part per million" meant that one-fifth of the carbon dioxide in the air I was breathing had been put there by humans.[13] Thirty years later, one-fifth had become one-third. Three hundred and forty-nine had become 408 parts per million. This was the air I and my family were breathing when we arrived in Stirling.

The concert was held in King's Park. This former hunting ground is on a floodplain in the shadow of Stirling Castle. The stonewalled castle sits atop a crag of solidified black magma and overlooks the northern limits of the Lowlands. The oblate form of the crag is a testimony to the steady southeastward flow of ice during the last glaciation. In mid-afternoon, we joined the rivers of fans which flooded the city streets and converged on the field below. It was an overcast day, but it was still. We were the lucky ones. Tickets had sold out in minutes.

I was on Islay when it happened. I was standing with a group of my students with my hand stretched out across sixty million years. My thumb was before and my index finger was after Snowball Earth. It was the very same geological boundary that Anthony had taken me to on the Holy Isle, not quite so spectacular but far easier to get to. The boundary can be followed along a small grassy hilltop valley. It is a narrow strip of green just below the top of a small heather-clad hill near the middle of the island. I call the place Snowball Earth Valley. I had explained how Earth's temperature plummeted down by 60 degrees before skyrocketing up by 80 degrees. With my outstretched finger on the shattered remains of a stromatolite. I talked about climate change. I drew parallels with what was happening today. I wondered if they understood. I did not.

My phone pinged. I left my words hanging in the air. I excused myself and walked to the other side of the hill from where I could see the mast and the mast could see me. I clicked on the link and found my way to the purchase button. I was in time. I was among the first 25,000. I bought four tickets.

I returned to Snowball Earth Valley and carried on talking about climate change.

We showed our tickets and entered the gates. We queued at the official merchandise stall and I spent eighty pounds on T-shirts. Then we staked out our patch. We were early, so we were quite far forward. Then we waited. There was excited anticipation in the air. The clans were gathering.

It was late afternoon when former lead singer Donnie Munro took the stage and filled the floodplain with the haunting words of *Dance Called America*. I was not the only one to shed tears. I was in the good company of a group of shinty players from Kinlochshiel on the Road to Skye. And if they shed tears, no one argues.

Runrig came on stage at 7:30 p.m. and the dance gained pace. They played slow ballads and fast reels. There were powerful Gaelic chants woven between gentle songs about beautiful places and times. The crowd knew them all. For three hours we were one in the music. Darkness fell and our 25,000 voices sang the song "Alba," which is the Gaelic name for Scotland, to the beating of the drum. In fear that the last dance had come, we shared the heart-breaking words of Loch Lomond. And then somewhere in the crowd a woman raised both of her hands above her head. The person beside her did the same. Then another followed. And another. And a wave of hands was born. It swept across the floodplain in rhythm with the dance. Then it flooded forward, rose, and broke against the barrier around the stage. We had become the tsunami.

We were the wave of destruction that was pounding the natural world into oblivion.

Bha mi ann means I was there.

The words were written across the back of the t-shirt of the man who stood in front of me in the queue for check-in at Edinburgh Airport.

So was I.

It was my last dance.

Figure 10.1 *The Last Dance at Stirling Castle, Scotland.*

11

2020

It was a very different world. The coronavirus had swept around the world in relentless waves, exposing global inequalities each time it passed.

The first wave reached Stockholm only days before I was scheduled to begin the two-day rail journey from Stockholm Central Station to Edinburgh Waverly. It would have been my fifth time by rail.

I had made the decision to fly less because I am in the privileged position of being able to. It makes sense; greenhouse gas emissions from flying are around five times higher than going by train.[1] But rail travel is a luxury. It is expensive. It takes more time. This is time few people have. I have time and I have money, so I can choose to go by rail.

I was back on Islay when I made the decision to fly less (I had flown there). I was with a small group of students in Snowball Earth Valley. It was the moment I realized that my students understood more than I did.

There was beauty all around me. Fields carrying the corrugated marks of the forgotten runrig system stretched out far below me. Towering above me, I could see the quartz-capped mountains of Jura glistened like snow in the hazy sunlight. The exquisite blue ocean wrapped around every headland and filled every cove of this island paradise. It was the legacy I wanted to pass on to my children.

In the rock face in front of me was the same geological boundary that I had abandoned to buy tickets to my last dance. In front of me was Snowball Earth. It was no more than a pencil-thin line. Below it was whitish-gray limestone crowned with bluish-gray stromatolite mounds. Above it were the same scenes of destruction I had witnessed on the Holy Isle. I recognized the same chaotic mixture of chunks of frozen land, with broken pieces of stromatolites. Anastomosing between them was the same poisonous orange foam of solidified carbon dioxide. In a layer of rock, no thicker than I am tall, I witnessed once more our planet freezing over in its entirety for sixty million years before plunging into a spiral of catastrophic meltdown.

My students made sketches and took notes. Then, I beckoned them forward to look more closely at the rock face. Each of them looked for a while before walking away. Eventually only one student remained. He was an eighteen-year-old from northern Sweden. He was fixated on one of the stromatolite mounds. Its upper surface was fractured. The fractures were filled with solid orange foam. He turned to look at me. The light was behind him, but I am sure that I could see tears in his eyes.

"Is it happening again?"

I did not know how to answer. Snowball Earth could not happen again. The surface of the Earth is no longer barren. It is covered by plants. It can no longer reflect so much of the radiation that comes from the Sun back into space. The giant mirror that triggered Snowball Earth no longer exists. But I knew that this is not what he was asking. He was asking about climate change. The likeness with the aftermath of Snowball Earth is not the magnitude of change. It is the speed of change. And it is speed of change that causes mass extinctions. My own best estimate for the aftermath of Snowball Earth is somewhere between 5,000 and 10,000 years for every 1 degree of warming.² This is how much Earth has warmed in the fifty years since I was born.³

I answered the only way I could. Honestly.

"Probably."

Finally, I too understood what it meant. That pencil-thin line on the rock face in front of me could be our time. I too found tears in my eyes. They were for the stromatolites of the past and for the children of the future.

On the day my train would have departed, the prime minister of Sweden addressed the nation. The address was solemn and powerful. There were overtones of Churchill in his words. He told us to ready ourselves. There would be suffering. There would be fear. Some would be forced to say farewell to their loved ones. Freedoms we took for granted would be taken away from us. It was a crisis. We needed to act responsibly for ourselves, for others, and for our country.

We were not ready. In our small country, more than five thousand people died in the first wave.⁴ Most were elderly, and some died alone. We were too late. The first reports of a new coronavirus in Wuhan were in mid-January. The first case in Sweden was confirmed on January 31. During the sport week holiday, which is in early March, we were advised not to travel to Italy. Five days later, Covid-19 was declared a pandemic by the World Health Organization.⁵ Our first death was on the same day.

In the spring of 2020, humanity was standing on that beach watching as the first wave of the pandemic advanced toward us. We did not run. It was not the first time we had been threatened by a coronavirus. It had happened before. The first case of SARS-CoV-1 was reported in Guangdong on November 16, 2002. In the months that followed, more than 700 people died in eleven countries.

Eighteen months later, on May 18, 2004, a statement was published by the World Health Organization claiming that it had been more than three weeks since the last case was placed in isolation.[6] The chain of transmission was broken. We had won.

We did not win against SARS-CoV-2.

I was fortunate. None of my family suffered severe illness. Lockdown swathed our city in a curtain of silence. The streets were empty. The criss-cross patterns of contrails were gone from the sky. It was as if time stood still. But it did not. All too often, the stillness was shattered by the wailing sound of an ambulance siren or the low rumble of a helicopter, vital reminders of the war being fought behind our hospital walls.

Nature carried on throughout the spring of 2020. The cherry trees bloomed in April, and candelabra blossoms filled the chestnut trees in May. In early summer, Sweden emerged from lockdown. There was talk of a second wave, but it was not upon us. There was also talk of a vaccine. There was hope. Families ventured out. There were cautious reunions, mostly out-of-doors. It was a beautiful summer, and I, among many others, learned to appreciate my near surroundings. The frantic rush to far-off places for a handful of days crammed full of must-see attractions bracketed on either end by airport stress was replaced with the peaceful calm of exploring our own 2-billion-year-old country.

The respite was short-lived. The second wave came in the autumn. We entered 2021, but 2020 did not end. As the fireworks of Hogmanay filled a snowless winter sky, Sweden's number of deaths passed from four to five digits.

Globally, SARS-CoV-2 took two million lives in 2020.[7]

One year after the first outbreak in Wuhan, we began mass vaccination. The rapidity with which a new approach to vaccination made it from the laboratory to mass usage was among the greatest achievements of modern science. Its effect was fast. The third wave, which swept across Sweden in the spring of 2021, was less deadly. The chance of dying fell by a factor of 4.

In the face of crisis, humanity had risen, but our rising triggered the deadliest wave of all. The wave of injustice.

The coronavirus attacked rich and poor with equal ferocity. However, vaccines were not shared out equally. While boosters were being given to people in high-income countries, fewer than 10 percent of people in low-income countries had received a single dose.

I live in a high-income country. I am party to that injustice.

That same injustice is a hallmark of the climate crisis. It is a fact that the richest half of the world stand for more than 80 percent of carbon dioxide emissions.[8] It is also a fact that the poorest half of the world are far more vulnerable to the cruellest impacts of climate change.[9]

The lockdown of 2020 caused a 7 percent fall in emissions.[10] It was unprecedented. Never before had our emissions fallen so massively.

One year before, our emissions of geological carbon reached 9.9 billion tons.[11] Never before had we burned so much ancient life. Half of this carbon was shared between the oceans and the land. The other half ended up in the air. Put another way, we wrapped our entire planet in a 4-centimeter-thick blanket made of carbon dioxide from the geological past.[12] The blanket we added in 2020 was three millimeters thinner.

Naively, we looked to the Mauna Loa Observatory hoping to see some kind of dent in the Keeling curve. We hoped that the fruits of our labor would somehow overcome a century spent abusing the air that we breathe. Our hopes were in vain. The signal of enforced lockdown was too small to be seen. It was lost in the margin of error.

Even if the fall in emissions brought about by lockdown restrictions failed to meet our naïve expectations, we learned that, as a species, we have what it takes to overcome the climate crisis.

We learned that we are fully capable of change when faced with a crisis that we can relate to. We accepted losses of freedom that we would never have accepted had we not been afraid of either dying ourselves or being the reason that someone else died. We acted decisively for the collective good. And above all, we learned that we are capable of care between generations.

Elderly people were at far greater risk of dying from Covid-19. The risks of dying or even of severe illness were much lower among the young. Nevertheless, millions of young people followed guidelines and stayed at home when they were sick, washed their hands regularly, and kept distance from one another. The young acted to protect the elderly. It was a beautiful example of care between generations.

The same principle underpins solutions to the climate crisis. All that it takes is for older generations to show the same care for the young as younger generations showed for the elderly during the pandemic. And I am sure that we would show this care if we felt that it really was necessary, not only in our heads, but also in our hearts. If we felt the same sense of crisis as we did on March 11, 2020, when the World Health Organization declared that the coronavirus disease was a pandemic, we would surely act.

But we don't. As adults, we can speak about the existential nature of the climate crisis, but we struggle to relate to what this actually means.

Our children, on the other hand, see the climate crisis differently. They not only understand it. They relate to it. For our children, mass extinction has real meaning. It will engulf them all. It will consume all that is beautiful in the world. They can see the tsunami wave. They can see how big it is and how fast it is moving. Perhaps this is why they acted before we did.

Figure 11.1 *Artist's reflection on the climate crisis. Artwork: Emmy Skelton Kockum*

12

Climate Live

The climate movement that began with one lone girl sitting in Parliament Square endured lockdown. Global strikes moved online. The voices of millions of children were not silenced by the coronavirus. And as its waves receded, flickering sparks came together again. Their united voices were heard once more. The movement was catching fire. Again.

I think that it is fair to say that the movement started in Sweden, even if its roots go back as far as the poetry of the Romantic Era, if not further. It is perhaps unsurprising given Sweden's history of social movements, which goes back to the Revival, Temperance and Labor Movements of the 1800s. These movements were largely successful. They reformed religion, created a safer alcohol culture, brought about the eight-hour working day, and set the stage for democracy.

The climate movement grew quickly. Thirteen months after Greta Thunberg sat alone outside the Swedish Parliament with a handwritten sign on which was written *Skolstrejk för klimatet*, over four million people took to the streets on the first day of the third global climate strike, making real her statement that *no one is too small to make a difference*.

Climate Live was a part of that movement, but it was not a strike. It was a concert arranged by young activists for climate justice. It was among the first public gatherings after lockdown. It was unknowingly timed such that it fell within what turned out to be a brief lull between the third and fourth coronavirus waves. Climate Live had a clear message for policymakers: *Can you hear us now?*

The stage was set in the King's Garden. It was October. Barren cherry trees flanked both sides of the five-hundred-year-old meeting place. The sky was clear, and a chill wind cut across the concrete garden. It did nothing to deter a growing crowd of climate activists. It was a matter of weeks before political leaders would gather in Glasgow for the Conference of the Parties (COP) for the purpose of making decisions about our future.

The youth activists asked me to speak. They wanted a scientist to talk about climate.

I know some of them. I guess that is why they asked me. I sat with them on a few occasions at Parliament Square and talked with them about the science behind the climate crisis. They were concerned. And their concerns are justified. It is easy to glorify them and to forget that the young activists are just ordinary children who want to do what ordinary children do. But they can't, because they know, and understand the enormity of the climate crisis. They know and understand that it will engulf them and all that they hold dear. They know that this will happen in their own lifetimes unless we act. Yet the world around them does not act. The young have no choice but to be activists.

I felt honored that they asked me, and at the same time, I felt uncertain how to respond.

As a geologist, I never thought of myself as a climate scientist. Geologists study rocks. Meteorologists study weather. The textbook definition of climate, which I wrote about earlier—an average of weather over a period of thirty years—comes from meteorology, not geology. The climates geologists speak of are more akin to the *climes* of Aristotle. There is an underlying sense of permanency (or at least millions of years).

Today, the meteorological, and geological definitions of climate are converging. For a geologist, climate is the result of a playoff between volcanic eruptions adding carbon dioxide to the atmosphere and weathering of granite taking it away again. This playoff is governed by continental drift. Continents breaking apart cause more volcanic eruptions, carbon dioxide is added to the atmosphere, and the climate warms. Continents colliding forms mountains, exposing vast quantities of fresh granite to the atmosphere. This granite weathers, and the climate cools. None of this happens quickly. Continental drift can change the amount of carbon dioxide in the atmosphere so as to warm or cool the climate by about 1 degree every three million years.[1] By burning fossil fuels, we have added carbon dioxide to the atmosphere so quickly that the climate has warmed by 1 degree in 50 years.[2] This is a geological change caused by humans, which has happened since I was born. Put another way, humans have become *geological actors*. This is why geologists have become climate scientists.

Even if I had been made a climate scientist by human actions, I was (back then) not a climate activist. The role of climate scientists was clearly defined. We create and communicate fundamental knowledge about climate. Our main way of communicating is by writing academic papers. These are not only for our peers. They do reach policymakers. There is an established mechanism whereby this happens. It is by way of the communication channel that was founded by the United Nations Environmental Program and the World Meteorological Organization, the IPCC.

The objectives of this United Nations body are:

i. *to make assessments of available scientific information on climate change;*

ii. *to make assessments of environmental and socio-economic impacts of climate change; and*

iii. *to formulate response strategies to meet the challenge of climate change.*[3]

Our academic papers constitute the available scientific information which is assessed in each of the IPCC's reports.

The reason I agreed to speak is the simple truth that after thirty years of IPCC reports, someone had finally understood them. It was not the policymakers for whom the reports were intended. The continued rise of emissions made that clear. It was our children.

The first song at Climate Live was written by Pink Floyd. I didn't like it, because its message that we don't need education was wrong. Yes, we do. If ever there was a time when we need education, it is now.

I was to be on stage at 7 p.m. I needed to be back stage thirty minutes before. The outdoor arena was already packed. It felt unseasonably cold. The audience crowded together for warmth. There was a wonderful feeling of normality. It was as if the pandemic had never happened.

There were speeches by young activists from Sweden and by activists who had traveled there from the Global South. They used the abbreviation MAPA which means "Most Affected People and Areas." The purpose of MAPA is to make the communities most affected by climate change and marginalized communities more visible. The MAPA activists had come to Sweden before continuing on to Glasgow. They spoke about political failings. They spoke about types of social injustice that I was unaware existed. They spoke about a divided world that must be united.

Then there was another song. Climate Live was like a rock concert, but at the same time it was very different.

At 6:30 p.m., I weaved my way through the crowd until I found the backstage entrance. I saw one of the young activists whom I know. Her name is Sophia. I will tell you more about her later on. I felt relieved. She ushered me through a makeshift barrier, up onto a platform, and down a set of stairs to the preparation area, which was underneath the stage. I found myself in a room full of musicians. Some were really famous. I felt completely out of place. I found a corner and rehearsed my lines. It was a way of calming my nerves.

The act before me was a dance. Two young activists—Andreas and Greta—reminded the audience that they are ordinary children. From side-stage, I watch this scene of joy, which I did not want to follow. But my name was still called. I walked on stage. I was trembling. I was really nervous. I wanted to hold the microphone in both hands to steady myself, but I needed my other hand to hold my notes. One of the presenters introduced me. She used my academic title. This concerned me. My title told my audience that I am a geochemist and a petrologist. The first part is fine, but would my audience understand the difference between a petrologist who studies rocks and a petroleum geologist who searches for oil? I hoped so.

The presenters would ask me four questions. I knew what they would be and I had rehearsed my answers.

At first, I was blinded by the spotlights, but as my eyes adjusted, I began to see my audience. My concerns faded away. Any resemblance of a rock concert was gone. I was facing hundreds of children. Many were tearful. I saw hope and I saw trust. To them, I am a scientist, and

Figure 12.1 *Andreas Magnusson and Greta Thunberg onstage at Climate Live in October 16, 2021 at the King's Garden, Stockholm, Sweden. Photographer: Adam Karls Johansson*

my task was simple. It was to tell them the truth. I didn't want to. But I did. I had no choice.

I told them that we see all the signs. Heat waves. Floods and droughts. Wildfires. Melting ice and rising seas. The wave is on the horizon. It is coming closer.

I told them that the climate crisis is here and now.

I called on policymakers to act.

I was staring into the eyes of many hundreds of scared children, and I spoke of care between generations. I spoke of hope and I tried to feel it.

Then I fell silent. I raised one hand while holding on to the microphone. I am not sure why. Then my audience responded. In front of me, a sea of hands rose. A new wave was forming. It was a wave of empowerment. For a split second, I really did feel hope.

13

Heat Waves

There will be more heatwaves in a warmer world.

Heatwaves that would have occurred once every fifty years in a climate unaffected by humans will likely occur every year in a 4-degree warmer world.[1] Heatwaves will become a way of life.

When I was a child, heatwaves were natural disasters. Today, most heatwaves are not natural at all. They are man-made. They are by-products of burning fossil fuels.

Natural disasters are innocent. They are "Acts of God." The 2004 tsunami meant no harm. It was a natural outcome of a major earthquake occurring on the ocean floor. Nevertheless, more than 283,000 people lost their lives when it swept across the Indian Ocean.[2] But nobody was to blame. It just happened.

The same can no longer be said for heatwaves. We burn fossil fuels. Burning fossil fuels adds carbon dioxide to the air. Adding carbon dioxide to the air strengthens the greenhouse effect. Strengthening the greenhouse effect makes the Earth hotter.[3] There are more heatwaves on a hotter Earth. We are to blame. But we fail to follow this chain of logic each time we burn fossil fuels ourselves or each time we make a decision that means that fossil fuels are burned by someone else. The chain is too long. But we are still to blame. Heatwaves are man-made.

The magnitude of the earthquake that caused the 2004 tsunami was 9.1.[4] It was the largest earthquake in forty years. It released energy that had accumulated along the plate boundary between India and Eurasia for over 300 years. Twelve minutes after it occurred, seismologists could calculate preliminary earthquake parameters, which told them that it was big enough to trigger a tsunami. The Pacific Tsunami Warning Center issued a warning, but it soon became clear that the areas covered by the early warning system would not be affected. The warning was withdrawn. The nations which surround the Indian Ocean received no warning. None of them participated in the early warning system. They do now.

There were plenty of early warnings before the first man-made heatwave I experienced. There was ample time to prepare. The UK Meteorological Office issued its first-ever red warning for exceptional heat on July 18 and 19, 2022. The UK Health Security Agency issued a level four heat health alert. The heat wave would last for forty-eight hours, and then it would become cooler. It would not only be hot during the daytime. It would also be hot at night. This made it more dangerous, because there would be no pause for "cooling off." The heat wave would need to be endured without relief. The warning was clear. It would be hottest in London and eastern England. These would be no ordinary "sunny days." The public was advised to stay indoors with window blinds down. I wonder how this worked if one lived in a 10-square-meter apartment in a tower block with no air conditioning. The railway network readied itself for chaos. The railways in Britain are not designed for 40 degrees, because 40 degrees does not happen in Britain. The concern was that rails would warp in the heat. The damage could be permanent. Train services on July 18 and 19 would run at reduced speed or not at all.

I was staying in my childhood home in the Scottish Highlands when I first heard about the heat wave. It was hard to believe that it was coming. The weather was so "normal." As children growing up in the Highlands, we would call "55 degrees and raining" normal for summertime. We were not far off. Fifty-five degrees Fahrenheit is 13°C. Back then, normal for July ranged from 11 to 18 degrees. By 2022, normal had become hotter. Its range extended to 19 degrees. How can "normal" be a moving target?

Normal has a meteorological definition. According to the World Meteorological Office, a "climate normal" is an average of weather conditions for a particular location over a thirty-year period. The standard period which meteorologists used back then started in 1961 and ended in 1990. This was the thirty-year period meteorologists compared with to decide if the weather on a particular day was normal or not. Back then, climate normals[5] were updated every thirty years, meaning that the next climate normal would be from 1991 to 2020. Now, because the climate is changing so fast, climate normals are updated every ten years. This all makes sense from a meteorological point of view, but this sliding scale of normality causes a lot of confusion. For example, a heatwave which would have been classified as extreme when compared with the 1961 to 1990 climate normal might be classified as "normal" if it was compared with the hotter 1991 to 2020 climate normal.

However, it did not matter which climate normal one compared with. Forty degrees in Britain was extreme.

I was fortunate. I was booked on an afternoon Eurostar from London St. Pancras to Amsterdam, by way of the Channel Tunnel, on July 16. This was two days before the heatwave was forecast to arrive. I would miss it. And indeed, I did. As the temperature began to rise in London, I was in Amsterdam. And by the time that the heat wave was encroaching on Amsterdam, I was in Hamburg.

The heat wave did not catch up with me until I had reached Sweden, and when it got there, its temperature peak was lower. It was *only* 37.2 degrees and it only lasted for a few hours. It was nevertheless the hottest day experienced in Sweden in seventy-five years. I was out-of-doors when it peaked at 5 p.m. It was not unpleasant. But nor was it normal. It felt wrong. It was a different kind of hot than I had experienced in Sweden. I had experienced hotter elsewhere, but never in the North. The scientist in me told me that it was "just weather," but the human being in me was uneasy.

The heatwave, which I found "not unpleasant," killed more than two thousand people in the UK.[6] This was the number of excess deaths, of which more than one thousand were among over-65s. Many deaths were due to heart attacks, breathing difficulties and, among elderly people with dementia, dehydration. This was because the part of the brain that tells you that you're thirsty doesn't always work in dementia sufferers.

One week after it happened, weather attribution scientists could show that the temperature peak, which ended up at 40.3°C, was "extremely unlikely" without human-caused climate change.[7] They found that "climate change made the heatwave at least ten times more likely than it would have been without human-caused greenhouse gas emissions."

The feeling of uneasiness that I had experienced as the heatwave passed over Stockholm had a statistical basis. The heatwave was (almost certainly) man-made.

The second man-made heatwave I experienced was far scarier.

It was on New Year's Day.

It was scary because it went almost entirely unnoticed, simply because it happened in January. I was in southern Sweden at the time. I had gone for a walk in the pine woods by the sea. It was early afternoon. There was a soft wind blowing onshore. The Sun was close to the horizon, and it was 12°C. This would have been normal had it been early summer. It was a strange feeling. It was both pleasant and terrifying.

The scary part was not the mildness of the weather. It was how we responded.

We enjoyed it. We walked in the woods. We went for a run. We rode bikes. Children played on the beaches. We returned home to celebrate the New Year with our families and friends. It was a perfect afternoon. But it wasn't. The wave was approaching, hidden below the horizon. It filled me with terror.

By the time that you read this chapter, my guess is that the UK heatwave of 2022 will have been forgotten. It will have been surpassed many times over by ever more powerful heatwaves. Indeed, a time will come, even in northern countries, when we will fear the summer months and winters will become a time of respite.

14

Floods and Droughts

There will be more severe floods and worse droughts in a warmer world.

It is far easier to predict rising temperatures than to know how much and where it will rain. But we do know that hotter air holds more moisture, so we can expect it to rain harder in a warmer world. We also know that weather patterns shift in a warmer world, so we can expect it to become wetter in some parts of the world and drier in others.

In its sixth assessment report, the IPCC stated that the kind of heavy rain that causes flooding will likely occur two or three times more often in a 4-degree warmer world and that it is likely that droughts will occur four times more often.[1] The IPCC used the word "likely." This acknowledgment of uncertainty is sometimes met with skepticism, but it is vital. It would be unethical for scientists to speak of certainty unless we know beyond all reasonable doubt that a statement is certain. What is critical is to be aware that "likely" means "likely." When reading the word "likely" in a scientific statement, I suggest envisaging the same word in a sentence that is easier to relate to. For example: It is likely that the plane you are about to board will crash. Would you board that plane? When scientists write "likely," we mean it.

I have never experienced real flooding, so I don't know what it feels like to watch as all that one has worked for, all one's worldly possessions, are washed away. I cannot begin to imagine what it feels like to watch as photo albums with pictures of generations of loved ones are forever destroyed by floodwater as it relentlessly rises around one's home, or to watch as the land that one depends on for food is submerged and ruined beyond repair. And I have never witnessed a flash flood wash loved ones away.

Nor have I been adversely affected by a drought. If a drought causes crops to fail in one part of the world, I buy food from another. I am not affected. My livelihood is not ruined. I do not go hungry.

I have never experienced this because of where and when I was born. I am privileged by chance. I was born in the Global North. I do not feel vulnerable to the negative impacts of global warming. This is because I am not vulnerable. Not yet.

When I read that 1.7 million homes were destroyed by flooding in Pakistan[2] and that four million people face starvation because of prolonged droughts in northeastern Africa[3] and that both events were made more likely because of climate change caused by humans, I feel sad for a while. Sometimes I feel guilty. But then I forget and move on. I find it hard to relate to a crisis in a place where I have never been. It seems so far away.

I find it difficult to make the connection between burning fossil fuels in the Global North and people starving or losing their homes in the Global South. But the connection is real. Burning fossil fuels adds carbon dioxide to the air. Adding carbon dioxide to the air strengthens the greenhouse effect. Strengthening the greenhouse effect makes the Earth hotter. There are more floods and droughts on a hotter Earth. I know all this in my mind, but I do not relate to it in my heart.

But I must. Indeed, we all must. This is climate justice.

There are good reasons for Sweden's young activists having chosen climate justice as the theme for Climate Live: The richest half of the world's population stands for more than 80 percent of global carbon dioxide emissions,[4] but it is not the richest half of the world who are worst affected by climate change. Most people who have suffered because of flooding or droughts reside in low-income countries. Weather attribution studies show statistically that floods and droughts are made more likely or worsened (or both) because of climate change caused by humans.[5] The link is there. It is real. The young are sometimes better than the old at relating to all of this. They are sometimes better at seeing beyond numbers to real human suffering.

Weather attribution may have a central part to play in our pursuit of climate justice. This rapidly expanding research field is about pinning extreme weather events such as floods and droughts on climate change caused by humans. Weather attribution studies address questions which must be addressed. When is it climate change? When is it "just weather?" They make it possible for scientists to address such fundamental questions with statistics. How much greater was the risk of an extreme weather event having occurred because of climate change caused by humans? The use of the word "risk" is important because it opens questions about responsibility. Who is responsible if a human being dies prematurely in a heatwave which was made more likely by greenhouse gas emissions? Was it an "Act of God" or willful manslaughter? If so, by whom?

When we burn fossil fuels in the Global North, are we responsible for deaths in the Global South?

Even if it hurts, we must face these questions head-on. Facing them may help us move forward on the pathway to climate justice.

Droughts cause more than crop failures. Combined with heatwaves, droughts set the stage for wildfires. This "stage" is called "fire weather." This is weather that is conducive to wildfires. Fire weather is hot, dry, and windy. In fire weather, a lightning strike, or a careless mistake can be all that is needed to start a wildfire. There will be more fire weather in a warmer world.[6]

Wildfires can be good. They encourage biodiversity. Wildfires cause small disturbances which allow for a more diverse fauna to thrive. Without wildfires, one species might take over at the expense of others. This is one of nature's many ways of regulating itself. Wildfires are part of an elegantly balanced and finely tuned natural system. Humans have upset this balance, not only by making the Earth hotter, but also by exploiting the land in a careless manner.

The consequences are devastating.

Wildfires in peatlands and rainforests release vast quantities of carbon dioxide to the air. Adding carbon dioxide to the air strengthens the greenhouse effect. Strengthening the greenhouse effect makes the Earth hotter and more susceptible to wildfires.

This kind of self-perpetuation is called positive feedback. This nomenclature is misleading as there is nothing "positive" about it. But scientists call it a positive feedback because it reinforces itself. Global heating causes a change of events which leads to more global heating.

The opposite is a negative feedback. The manner in which the weathering of granite stabilizes Earth's climate is a negative feedback. Warming causes a chain of events (granite weathers faster, more carbon dioxide is removed from the air, and the greenhouse effect weakens) which leads to cooling, and cooling causes a chain of events (granite weathers more slowly, less carbon dioxide is removed from the air, and the greenhouse effect strengthens) which leads to warming.

A general rule for the climate is that negative feedbacks are good and positive feedbacks are bad.

I have never experienced a wildfire, but a close friend has. Her story was not dramatic, but it touched me because it felt so real.

The wildfire was in Portugal. It was in 2017. It was preceded by a massive heat wave with peak temperatures above 40 degrees. Weather attribution scientists calculated that the heat wave was ten times more likely to have occurred because of global warming caused by humans.[7] On a single afternoon, 156 fires erupted across Portugal's mountainous hinterland. They were most probably ignited by "dry lightning." This is lightning produced by thunderstorms which do not produce rain.

My friend was traveling from Lisbon to Madrid on an overnight train called Lusitania. She was alone with her child. The railway line runs quite far south of the place where the fires started, but as night fell, the fires spread southwards.

She knew that something was wrong when the train came to a halt. They were at a station. Somewhere. It was the middle of the night. The train crew woke all of the passengers. They alighted the train and waited in the darkness. Buses came and collected them. The buses took a different route that circumnavigated the place where the fires were burning.

The first thing my friend noticed of the wildfires was the smell of burning. It was faint at first, but it grew stronger. And stronger. Then there was an eerie red glow on the horizon. Then, faraway in the distance, she could see the fire itself.

She spoke of finding comfort in car headlights coming toward her. As long as there were headlights coming in the opposite direction, the road ahead must still be open. This touched me because I could relate to what she said. I remember crossing the Highlands in a raging blizzard and feeling comforted by headlights coming toward me. The road was open. It was not closed by snow.

My friend spoke of feeling unprepared. Had she known, she would have charged her phone. Had she known, she would not have been there at all. Her phone battery was nearly dead. Who should she call? Who needed to know? Who would react calmly? And then there was the bottle of water she was carrying. It was small. It was nearly empty. It needed to be enough for both of them. What would she do if it wasn't?

One hundred and seven people in Portugal and Spain died in the 2017 wildfires. My friend was not one of them. Nor was her child. They both arrived safely in Madrid, but the climate crisis became real for her that night, and that reality will never leave her.

Others were less fortunate. People's homes, vast areas of farmland, and numerous hard-earned livelihoods were consumed by the flames. It was all counted. It all became a part of the statistics of climate change. But what about the animals? Nobody counts the number of animals that die in a wildfire, but they are equally dead.

Since the 2017 wildfires in Portugal and Spain, I do not remember a year without wildfires. Nor do I remember a year that was untouched by climate change caused by humans. The climate is no longer normal. Six years on, I found myself in a rainswept Sweden while wildfires raged across southern Europe. Again. These particular fires were caused by a heatwave with peak temperatures that would have been virtually impossible were it not for humans having warmed the planet by burning fossil fuels.[8] This man-made heatwave was named Cerberus after the multiheaded dog which guarded the gates to Hades. It was one of the first named heatwaves in history. It will not be the last.

Worst hit were Spain, Italy, Greece, and Cyprus.

While Athens was burning, I was walking in the streets of Stockholm. It was raining. It was soft, gentle, and kind. The city was calm and still. The temperature peaked at 17 degrees. I walked past a Greek restaurant. It was owned by two brothers who are as Swedish as they are Greek. It had been there for over twenty years. I spoke with them about the wildfires. I asked if they had family who were affected. They did not. Then one of them asked me a question, which I could not bring myself to answer. He asked me when it all would end.

It won't end.

Two years after Cerberus ravaged Europe, wildfires struck California. It was January. As I walked past that same Greek restaurant enjoying a flurry of snow in a brief flirtation with winter, Los Angeles was on fire. As that month came to a close, wildfires had killed twenty-eight people and burned down more than 16,000 buildings in California. Even before the fires had stopped burning, weather attribution scientists managed to show statistically that the wildfires were made more likely because of climate change caused by humans.[9]

None of this will end. This is just the beginning.

15

Melting Ice and Rising Seas

Ice will melt and the seas will rise in a warmer world.

The Arctic Ocean is projected to be practically ice-free by the middle of this century.[1] This means that polar bears will no longer be able to prey on seals. Polar bears will be forced to make dens on land and find other species to prey on. Because seals are among the only prey which can provide the fat that polar bear cubs need for their survival, many of them will suffer and die.

Continued ice loss over the century is virtually certain for the Greenland Ice Sheet and likely for the Antarctic Ice Sheet. Ice sheets are made of freshwater (not saltwater), so as the Greenland Ice Sheet melts, huge quantities of freshwater will pour into the North Atlantic Ocean. This may weaken ocean circulation. This is because freshwater is not as heavy as saltwater, so it does not sink to the bottom of the ocean like saltwater does, and it is the sinking of saltwater in the North Atlantic Ocean that is the pump that drives ocean circulation. Circulation of ocean water creates the conditions needed for all different kinds of sea creatures to live and flourish. Collapse of ocean circulation will mean that many of them will suffer and die.

Mountain glaciers will carry on melting until they are gone. This will remove the habitats of various kinds of insects.[2] Mayflies are among them. They support primary producers. These are organisms that acquire energy from sunlight by photosynthesis. They form the base of the food chain. The mayflies support them by burrowing into sediments at the bottom of glacial lakes and freeing up nutrients, which stimulate photosynthesis. These harmless and beautiful winged beings will suffer and die as their homes disappear. They will no longer burrow into sediments and free up nutrients. The primary producers, which rely on these nutrients, will stop photosynthesizing. The fish that feed on them will have less food. They will go hungry. They too will suffer and die.

The melting of ice causes more ice to melt. This is because melting sea ice, ice sheets, and glaciers expose darker surfaces (sea and land), which are warmed faster by sunlight. This warming causes more ice to melt, exposing more dark surfaces, and causing more warming. This feedback continues until all the ice is gone.

The melting of ice sheets and glaciers causes sea level rise. It is not the only cause. The other one is the fact that water molecules move more energetically and take up more space in a warmer world. It is likely that the sea will have risen by a half meter or more by 2100, and a sea level rise of more than 15 meters within a few centuries can no longer be ruled out.[3] This would affect almost all coastal cities, and most cities are coastal.

Sea level rise is not fair. The sea does not rise faster in the richer countries of the Global North, which are responsible for 80 percent of carbon dioxide emissions.[4] To the contrary, some of those countries are largely unaffected by sea level rise. I live in one of them. Parts of Sweden are actually rising out of the sea.

My home city of Stockholm is built on land that has been rising out of the sea for more than 10,000 years and will carry on doing so for another couple of decades.

We know that much of Sweden is rising out of the sea because we find seashells in the Swedish hills. They were first remarked on by the scientist who gave us the Celsius temperature scale. In a paper which was published in 1743, Andrius Celsius wrote about a place near the small town of Uddevalla in southwestern Sweden, where curious banks of all kinds of seashells could be found 50 meters above the present-day level of the sea. In the same paper, he commented on Swedish place names, which told of past shorelines, bays, and headlands which were also far inland. He noted names of inland villages which were built around words such as "vik" which means bay, "sund" which means straits, and "holm" which means small island. His explanation for these curious findings was that the sea was "diminishing" fast enough to be measurable in a human lifetime. According to Celsius,[5] seawater evaporated to make clouds which produced rain. The rain fell on the land, but not all of it returned to the sea. Instead, some rainwater was captured by plants and used for photosynthesis. Thus, sea level was higher in the past and was falling and would continue to fall until the seas were gone.

Charles Lyell, who is famed for the principles, which geologists rely on to know that one rock is older than another one, did not agree with Celsius. In a paper that was published in 1835,[6] Lyell put forward another explanation for finding seashells far above present-day sea level in Sweden. He proposed that it was the land that was rising, not the seas that were falling. He claimed that the rising of the land was powered by some kind of "heat engine" in Earth's interior. The existence of such a "heat engine" had been proposed fifty years earlier by the geologist James Hutton in his *Theory of the Earth*. In his theory, Hutton spoke of old continents eroding away and being replaced by new ones, which rose out of the seas, forced upward by the power of heat. This cycle of rejuvenation was everlasting. In his own words: "... we find no vestige of a beginning—no prospect of an end."[7]

Today, we call on the Ice Age Theory to explain the rising of the land. This theory, which tells of massive ice sheets covering much of northern Europe, was proposed by Louis Agassiz in 1837[8] as an explanation for finding enormous boulders of foreign rocks in low-lying parts of Switzerland. Agassiz claimed that these "erratic boulders" could only have been carried to their present locations by the agency of ice. The connection to the rise of the land came much later. It was put forward by the Scottish scientist Thomas Jamieson in 1865.[9] He postulated that the ice sheets, which had covered northern Europe, weighed down on the land, pressing it downward into the mantle, which we now know to be soft and plastic in its behavior. The mantle would have made space by flowing away to the sides. And it would have flowed back again as the ice sheet melted away, pressing against the land from underneath and causing it to rise upward. This theory was not fully accepted until 1890, after the Swedish geologist Gerald De Geer had mapped out the raised shorelines,[10] which it sought to explain.

De Geer's maps were contoured for the rising of the land. On them, he was able to pinpoint the part of Sweden which had risen farthest and fastest and he postulated that this was where the thickest part of the ice sheet had been. This place is called the High Coast. It is a spectacular region of flat-topped mountains and steep-sided fjords. It is a place where one can find raised beaches surrounded by pine forests, more than 260 meters above the present-day Baltic Sea. These ancient shores, which flank mountains that were once islands, are the highest in the world. It is an eerie feeling to climb up to a mountain summit and walk out from the forest onto an open expanse of cobblestone ridges, each made of stones which had been rounded by waves lapping against the shore. Or to walk into a sea cave which has not heard the sound of those waves for over 10,000 years.

The High Coast continues to rise by one centimeter every year.[11] It is so fast that if one closes one's eyes, one can almost feel it.

Stockholm rises more slowly. This is because where the city is now, the ice sheet was thinner. Nevertheless, Stockholm rises by 5.5 millimeters every year.[12] But at the same time the sea is rising because of climate warming caused by humans. As I write these words, I know that the rising of the sea is slower than the rising of the land. But I also know that the sea is rising ever faster and that a time will come, most likely during my own lifetime, when Stockholm will start to sink back into the sea. And then the great lake of Mälaren, from which Stockholm takes its drinking water, will become a part of the Baltic Sea.[13] Freshwater will become saltwater and our drinking water will be gone.

Of course, because Stockholm is a wealthy city, its residents will not go without. Drinking water will be piped in from the great rivers that flow down from the western mountains or from another one of our great lakes. It will be expensive. There will be conflicts. But it will happen.

But freshwater is not all that will be gone. Stockholm is a city built on islands amid an archipelago, which consists of a few hundred more islands and many thousand tiny skerries. On some of them, one finds small red-painted wooden houses. These are summer homes. Many are built right by the shore and are safe there because the land is rising. These small red houses perched on granite skerries are symbolic of Stockholm. But their fate has been decided. They will disappear.

I know that I should care more about the countries that will disappear entirely in the rising seas, but I find it easier to relate to the small red houses on the skerries near my Swedish hometown. Many

Figure 15.1 *A shingle beach situated 200 meters above sea level on top of a mountain. High Coast, Sweden.*

of them are summer houses. Are they unnecessary luxuries that our planet cannot sustain or essential refuges from the frenetic chaos of city life which bring people closer to nature? I do not know, and it is not my place to pass judgment. But when I pass by one of them on the ferry to the island where I teach my students Lyell's principles of geology, I cannot stop myself from thinking that perhaps the small red house I am looking at was built by someone for someone. Maybe it was built by a grandparent for her grandchild to enjoy when she is no longer of this world. And I feel sad because I know that this will not happen because, one by one, each small red house will disappear beneath the waves.

Figure 15.2 *Traditional red summer house on a low-lying skerry in the Stockholm Archipelago, Sweden. This summer house will not survive sea level rise caused by human emissions of greenhouse gases.*

Stockholm will lose more than a few low-lying skerries in a warmer world. It will lose its winters.[14]

I can write this with some certainty because "winter" has a meteorological definition in Sweden. According to the Swedish Meteorological and Hydrological Institute, winter begins when average temperatures fall below 0°C on five consecutive days.[15]

When I immigrated to Stockholm, "normal" was that winter began in December. Now, winter begins in January.[16] And as my children venture out into a world of uncertainty, winter will begin in February, if it begins at all.

Indeed, statistics tell me that I will witness Stockholm's "end of winter."[17]

"End of winter" does not mean that it will not snow again. Nor does it mean that the lakes will never freeze over. It means that normal will no longer be snow. Normal will be sleet. And then normal will be rain. There will still be days when snowflakes fall gently on the city streets and fill chill air with glistening beauty, but such days will be few and far between. And then one such day will be the last one, but we will not know it at the time. Instead, we will look forward to another such day coming until we can no longer remember what we are looking forward to. Winter will fade away.

What will not change is winter darkness. The Sun will continue to set before 3 p.m. in the afternoon in the weeks before Christmas. And it will feel even darker without snow. But the end of winter has a far deeper meaning than the darkness it will bring to northern countries. It speaks of the poleward movement of climate zones and of the speed with which they are moving.

Climate zones resemble the *climes* of Aristotle. They are geographical regions with distinct climates. They define the habitats of living things. Each climate zone supports a plethora of plants and animals that have evolved to live together in a harmonious balance that is perfectly in phase with the climate of that region.

Climate zones are not stationary. In an Ice Age, climate zones move northward and southward in a rhythm that is set by the cyclical variations of Earth's orbit around the Sun and the tilt of its rotational axis that are called Milanković cycles. The northward and southward drift of climate zones should happen slowly. In a world unaffected by human-induced global heating, the speed at which the climate zones move seldom exceeds 50 meters per year. Because the natural movement of climate zones is slow, living things can either move with them or stay where they are and adapt as the climate changes. There is enough time.

Today, because of human-induced global heating, the climate zones are moving much faster.[18] They are moving too fast.

As I write these words, the climate zones that define the habitats of some tree species are moving poleward 400 meters every year. This is eight times faster than they should be moving. In the lifetime of a tree, its habitat might move poleward by several tens of kilometers. Can such trees keep pace? Can a tree disperse its seeds far enough so that its offspring take hold in a place that will still be livable when that tree grows old? Because if not, its offspring will perish.

Grassland habitats are moving even faster. They are moving poleward more than 600 meters every year. Can grasses disperse their seeds far enough and in the right direction so that they can carry on living? What will happen to the animals that live in those grasslands when the grass is gone? What will happen to animals that live among the broadleaf trees of the rainforest or among the coniferous trees of the boreal forests? Where will they go?

How will living things keep pace as their habitats race across the landscape? And as, one by one, species fail to keep pace, what will happen to the plants and animals which depend on them for the food they need to stay alive? And what will happen when a land-living species that does manage to keep pace with its own habitat finds itself at some northern or southern shore beyond which lies nothing but ocean? What will happen when a mountain dweller reaches a mountain summit?

The breakneck speed at which the climate zones are now moving causes plants and animals to die out because they cannot keep pace with their own habitats or the habitats of the other species upon which they depend for their own survival. At the end of this spiral of sorrow, we risk finding a sixth mass extinction.[19] This is why the climate crisis is a crisis of biodiversity. It is a crisis of live itself. It is existential.

We are the reason for this existential crisis. When we burn fossil fuels, we add carbon dioxide to the air. Adding carbon dioxide to the air strengthens the greenhouse effect. Strengthening the greenhouse effect makes the Earth hotter. On a hotter Earth, climate zones move faster. Plants and animals cannot keep pace. They die out. Their deaths mark the beginning of the end.

This is what the end of winter in northern cities really means. It is far more than darkness.

16

Niko

While I was still standing on the shore watching as the wave crested the horizon, Niko had already understood what it all meant. The heat waves. The floods and droughts. The wildfires. The melting ice and rising seas. Niko read the signs before I did. He saw the tsunami. He turned his back on it, and he started to run.

I first met Niko when I was a postdoctoral fellow working at sea. We were on Leg 173 of the Ocean Drilling Program.[1] The drillship Joides Resolution embarked from Lisbon on April 15, 1997. Her destination was Halifax, Nova Scotia. The crossing would take eight weeks because the 143-meter-long ship would stand still a few hundred kilometers offshore from Portugal to drill into the ocean floor at a place we named Hobby High after the fast-flying migratory falcons called hobbies, which we saw when we were there. At Hobby High, our scientific mission was to find out how oceans and continents were joined together in the plate tectonic puzzle that envelops the Earth.

Niko and I shared sleeping quarters. These were straightforward and functional. There was a bunk bed with two sleeping berths (I had the lower one), a small desk which we shared, a cupboard, and a bathroom in our quarters. Each sleeping berth had a curtain that one could pull across so as to have some privacy. I loved that curtain.

With it drawn across, I had my own space to read, write, or to think my own thoughts.

I worked nights, and Niko worked days, so I only spoke with him at changeover times, which were at midnight, and midday. As he finished his evening meal, I would arrive for breakfast. At the convergence of our shifts, we would brief each other on what we had found in the cores that had been brought up from the bottom of the sea. We had the same task. We were both petrologists, meaning that we know about rocks and what they are made of. Our task was to describe and identify the rocks and minerals in the cores. It was exciting beyond words. The rocks we were describing were from kilometers below the ocean floor. We were the first people on Earth to see them.

The drill, which chewed its way into the ocean floor, was enormous. I had never seen anything like it. The drill string hung from a 60-meter-tall derrick midship above the "moon pool" through which it plunged for several kilometers to the ocean floor far below. The drill bit consisted of four rotating heads centered on a hollow cylindrical shaft within which elegantly crafted pulleys and cables pulled meter-long segments of core from far below the ocean floor onto the ship, where scientists of all backgrounds waited eagerly to describe them. When it was time, we would hear the longed-for words "core on deck" called out on the ship's loudspeaker system. When we heard those words, we would drop everything and race to the core deck to crowd around as pieces of the puzzle we were working to solve were carefully placed in front of us on purpose-built tables on the core deck. We would then work around the core for many hours, sometimes days, carefully describing every centimeter. It was all very well organized. Each of us would focus on our predesignated task, never straying over to the tasks of others. When a core had been fully described to everyone's satisfaction, we would be given a chance to place flags out on the parts of the core which we would like to sample for further research after the end of the cruise. This gave shipboard scientists a head start writing papers about what we found out there, as scientists on land would only have access to the drill cores six months after the end of the cruise.

The place where we were drilling was not only named after migratory birds. It was named Hobby High because it was a high point on the seafloor. This was where our puzzle could be solved. Geophysicists told us that the conspicuous bulge on the seafloor marked the exact position where ocean and continent were joined together. Or they thought it did. But when we got there and looked at the cores from beneath the seafloor, we found no join.

Both my and Niko's knowledge about rocks told us that Hobby High was neither ocean nor continent. Nor was it something in between. It was simply a gap between the end of Europe and the start of the Atlantic Ocean. The jigsaw of tectonic plates which envelope the Earth did not fit together perfectly. There were gaps between them.[2]

I am not sure if it was I or Niko who was on the core deck when we found out that what we were looking for was not there at all. What I am sure of is that being a part of such an unexpected discovery shaped my future career. Finding nothing where we expected to find something gave me a story to tell. I told it at scientific conferences. I told it at invited talks. I told it when I interviewed for a professorship at Stockholm University. And I got the job. Hobby High paved a pathway forward for my career.

Looking back to the eight weeks I spent at sea, eight weeks of unforgettable excitement and eight weeks of counting days before I would first smell and then see dry land again, I cannot help wondering if hobbies still fly over this bulge on the seafloor or if they have been forced to change their migratory routes so as to keep pace with their moving habitats.

These exquisite falcons spend the winters in Africa and the summers in northern Europe. When I was at sea on Joides Resolution, hobbies would spend the summer months feasting on dragonflies in English wetlands. Now, hobbies are found in Scotland and their numbers are increasing.[3] This might seem like a good thing until one asks: What about their food supply? Will there be enough for them to eat? What happens when they reach Africa? Will there be enough food for them there? Maybe hobbies will thrive. Maybe they will be the winners. Maybe not. We don't know what will happen when our actions force plants and animals which have evolved to live together to move somewhere else. We are conducting an uncontrolled experiment on the planet, which is our home, our children's home, and the home of 8.7 million other species of living things.[4]

Maybe this is why, twenty-five years after the Joides Resolution reached Halifax, Nova Scotia, marking the end of Leg 173, Niko glued himself to a motorway.

Niko began his efforts to communicate about the climate crisis in the same way I did. We gave public lectures. In our separate countries and our different languages, we explained that our greenhouse gas emissions were making the Earth hotter. We spoke like scientists because we are scientists. We assumed that our audiences would believe what we were saying. This was because there were vast amounts of data presented in multiple IPCC reports that supported every statement that we made at any of our lectures. Yet our audiences seemed not to believe us, or at least our audiences did not act as if they believed us. This was new to us both. For the first time ever as scientists, we were faced with the reality that stating scientific facts was not enough.

We worked on our pedagogy. We found new ways of expressing the same facts so that they were easier to understand. We began walking the tightrope of conveying our own feelings and emotions in our talks. Would this undermine our words or make them stronger? Was it wise to mix scientific facts with human feelings? Or did our audiences want us to be the calming voices of reason that told them that it will be alright in the end? But what if the data told us that it would not be alright in the end? What if the data made us afraid for our own children's futures?

Then we changed arenas. We left our academic classrooms behind us and began speaking on the streets. We commented on actions made by politicians. We questioned their decisions. We wrote endless debate articles. Our arenas changed, but our message never did. Reduce emissions. Now.

Yet emissions continued to rise.

It became more and more scary. It was as if we were standing on that shore, screaming at the top of our voices with the tsunami wave in full view, but no one could hear us. They just carried on playing in the sand.

And, one by one, colleagues with whom I had written academic papers, all of them respected scientists, glued themselves to motorways. Niko was one of them.

17

Sophia

Sophia was three years old when the tsunami wave swept across the Indian Ocean. Yet she saw it coming before I did.

She grew up in Stockholm and went to high school in Lysekil. This is a small and picturesque town on the west coast of Sweden, about 100 kilometers north of Gothenburg.

She plays underwater rugby, a sport that is similar to rugby on land but played underwater. She is good at it. She competes for Sweden.

She cares about the sea and the beautiful creatures it contains. She cares about dolphins, orcas, and whales. She cares about small gray crustaceans, which live on the muddy floor of the Bothnian Sea. They are called *Saduria entomon*. They are predators. They feed on creatures that are smaller than themselves and also live on the seafloor. They form a vital part of the food chain upon which fish, such as cod, are dependent on. Their future in the Bay of Bothnia is threatened by global warming.[1]

Her love of sea creatures began early in life. As a child, she was fascinated by nature documentaries, especially ones about the sea. But with her fascination came a growing sadness. She began questioning the fairness of keeping sea creatures in captivity. She became steadily more concerned about our exploitation of the sea. It is not surprising that she studied marine biology in high school and that she wrote projects on overfishing and pollution. When speaking about how we are harming our planet and its oceans, she told me that it stays with her. She can't ignore it.

Her escape is K-pop (Korean pop music) and Korean culture. She sells ice cream in the summertime. She needs the money.

Sophia is both ordinary and extraordinary.

She was one of a small group of children who created Fridays for Future. This is the global movement that has mobilized millions of people across the world to speak out for climate justice. Its members are children and youths. Fridays for Future has an upper age limit of twenty-six.

In December 2018, Sophia visited her sister in Stockholm. While she was there, she participated in her first school strike. This was at Parliament Square in Stockholm, not far from where Greta Thunberg had sat down alone a few months earlier. There were hundreds of children there. She said it was both overwhelming and empowering.

Sophia began solo striking in January 2019. She sat down alone outside the municipal hall in Lysekil every Friday. The first people who sat with her were a small group of pensioners. Later on, she was joined by a few of her friends. Then more came. And more.

The movement grew larger. By the end of January, one month after fifteen-year-old Greta Thunberg had spoken at the twenty-fourth COPin Katowice, Poland, where she accused the world's leaders of stealing their own children's future, children were striking from school across Europe, Australia, and the United States. And on Friday March 15, 2019, children across the world walked out of school, and more than one million people in 128 countries[2] took to the streets for the first global climate strike, proving, in Greta's own words, that "no one is too small to make a difference."

Sophia moved to Stockholm in the autumn of 2019 to study biology and geology. I was one of her geology teachers. I still remember the first day of class. Sophia was sitting quite far back in the auditorium. I thought I recognized her from the climate strike which had taken place on Friday May 24, 2019. I was wrong. Sophia has a twin sister. It was her I had seen at the strike.

This second global climate strike was the first one I attended. It was only a few days after that fateful day when I had been teaching my students in Snowball Earth Valley on Islay, and I finally realized how we were harming the planet we live on. Later that same day, one of my students contacted me. She told me that a group of scientists was going to set up a "desk" at the strike. It would be called "Researchers' Desk." It was going to become a central part of my life, although I did not know it at the time. It was to be a place where concerned citizens could ask questions about climate change and get fact-based answers. We would neither overdramatize nor play it down. There would be street lectures. My student asked me if I would give one of them. She asked me to explain the basics of climate change. I did. In five minutes, I explained how Earth's climate is controlled by solar radiation, the albedo effect, and the greenhouse effect. I used a mirror to illustrate the albedo effect and a blanket to represent the greenhouse effect. Holding a chunk of granite in my hand, I explained how the slow weathering of rocks removes carbon dioxide from the air, maintaining a stable climate. I explained that by burning fossil fuels, we were upsetting that balance. I explained that this was causing global warming and that it was bad. Very bad. I sincerely doubt that anything I said to the small group of listeners justified the vast amount of carbon dioxide I added to the air with my rebooked flights from Islay, via London, to Stockholm.

Sophia looked furiously at me as I stood behind the podium in the lecture hall and began to explain the practicalities of the up-and-coming field excursion to Scotland that was an obligatory part of the course she was taking. I found out later that her look of fury was because she thought I was going to require her to fly. She told me later that she would have done so, because she valued her education, but she would not have liked it. Fortunately for both of us, I did not. In the summer after the second global climate strike, I had tried out the rail journey from Stockholm to Edinburgh and found that it was doable. The route crossed seven countries: Sweden, Denmark, Germany, Belgium, France, England, and Scotland; and with careful planning one could get it down to five changes. These were in Copenhagen, Hamburg, Cologne, Brussels, and London. My plan was to offer a rail option for students who preferred not to fly. Four students chose this option. Sophia was one of them.

While I was making seat reservations for the journey and while her fellow students were learning how to use a microscope to study rocks, Sophia was working with a small team of youths to plan a global week of climate action. The week would begin and end with global climate strikes on September 20 and 27, both of which were Fridays. The week of climate action was scheduled to coincide with the United Nations Climate Action Summit in New York City. Greta was at this meeting. She had crossed the Atlantic Ocean in a sailing boat to get there. This was the place where she held her famous "How dare you!" speech in which she accused the world's leaders of stealing her childhood dreams. In her speech, she spoke clearly about ecosystem collapse and mass extinction. She had listened to and understood the science.

While Greta was on the other side of the Atlantic Ocean, Sophia was playing a central role in coordinating the global climate strikes in Stockholm. She is a natural leader. She makes things work. Later on, she became the person who maintained contact with the police about the demonstrations. This was crucial because a hallmark of Fridays for Future was to act legally (with the exception of school strikes). Fridays for Future as an organization did not encourage its members to glue themselves to motorways. Sophia was also in charge of social media. Despite all this, Sophia passed her geology exam.

This was the global strike at which more than four million people, many of them children, took to the streets across the world.[3] It was on the first Friday of the global week of climate action. It was the largest climate demonstration in history. Two million people attended the second strike which ended the week of climate action, one week later.

Four years later, after briefly pausing her work with Fridays for Future, Sophia helped out once more because she was needed. She spoke of feeling a sense of guilt, even though she knew that she should not feel guilty. She said that she felt that if she was not speaking out, she was not doing enough. So, once again, she found herself coordinating a climate strike and speaking on stage in front of the masses. And once again, the numbers of demonstrators began rising. Five thousand people marched out of Parliament Square on Friday, September 22, 2023. It was the largest strike since the coronavirus pandemic. It was also the hottest September in recorded history. It beat the previous record for that month by an unprecedented 0.5 degrees, which one climate scientist spoke of as being "absolutely gobsmackingly bananas."

It breaks my heart when I think of young people like Sophia. As adults, we sometimes speak of these youths as "our hope." It is so wrong of us. The young should not be our hope. We should be our own hope and the hope of our children. Instead, we have placed an intolerable burden on the shoulders of our children. Those that understand the science have no choice other than to fight for their own futures and for the futures of all that is beautiful on the Earth.

The last time I spoke with Sophia, she had taken a pause from writing her thesis on oceans and climate. She was studying the Korean language. I asked her why. Her answer was that it is because it has nothing to do with climate.

18

Conference of the Parties

Sophia is a climate activist. So is Niko. So am I.

And even if our approaches to activism are different, our call is the same. Our call is for climate justice for our children, for children whose voices are not heard because of where they were born, for children whose voices are not heard because they have not yet been born, and for all the plants and animals that will share the future with them.

There is no "one-size-fits all" form of climate activism.

Some activists speak in auditoriums. Some march in demonstrations. Some write debate articles. Some strike from school. Some glue themselves to motorways. Some are activists in the silence of their hearts.

And then there are others who do not call themselves activists, but they act anyhow. They write the academic papers that guide our pathway forward. They drive negotiations. They fight relentlessly for crucial formulations in texts that must guide the world.

What works? Which actions make a difference?

I do not know, but what I am sure of is that united we are stronger.

As the climate crisis rises from behind the horizon and bears down upon us, we must hold one another's hands and face it together. Together we are powerful.

I witnessed this power at the twenty-sixth Conference of the Parties[1] (COP26). I witnessed it rising across the misty streets of Glasgow as 2021 came to a close.

The COP is the "supreme decision-making body" of the United Nations Framework Convention on Climate Change, which is abbreviated to UNFCCC and which was founded in Rio on May 9, 1992. This was shortly after the concentration of carbon dioxide in the atmosphere first exceeded its own planetary boundary of 350 parts per million.

The COP reviews progress made by its 197 parties toward achieving agreed on goals which are written down in the treaties of the UNFCCC. These treaties include the Paris Agreement of 2015 to hold "the increase in the global average temperature to well below 2°C above pre-industrial levels" and to pursue efforts "to limit the temperature increase to 1.5°C above pre-industrial levels."

The COP is held every year, and its presidency rotates among the five regions of the United Nations. It is either held in Bonn, which is the seat of the UNFCCC secretariat, or it is hosted by parties of the region in which the presidency resides. COP26 had been delayed by one year because of the coronavirus pandemic. During that one year the concentration of carbon dioxide in the atmosphere rose from 414 to 416 parts per million.[2]

The presidency's aim for COP26 in Glasgow was to "keep 1.5 degrees within reach." Their motivation was that the differences between a 2-degree warmer world and a 1.5-degree warmer are massive.[3] There are greater risks to people's health and livelihoods, food security, water supply, and biodiversity in a 2-degree warmer world. This is because heat waves, droughts, floods, and wildfires will happen more often, more ice well melt, and sea level will rise faster and further.

In addition to 120 world leaders, over 22,000 party delegates, and almost 4,000 media representatives, COP26 was attended by over 14,000 observers, mostly from nongovernmental organizations (NGOs). I belonged to one of them. Stockholm University.

I traveled from Sweden to COP26 by train. Others walked the same route. Their journey took months. My journey took only two days with one overnight in Hamburg and another on the night train from London to Scotland. The route was similar to the one I used for the field excursion to Scotland (via Copenhagen, Hamburg, Cologne, Brussels, and London), only that I continued from Edinburgh to Glasgow.

On the first day, my route took me across all three of the Danish Straits. These connect the Baltic Sea to the North Sea. It was possible to walk across each of them during some of the winters of the Little Ice Age, which is around the time that Descartes visited Kristina. Each strait is crossed by one of the great bridges, each of which is many kilometers long, each iconic, and each represents an enormous feat of engineering. These bridges bring Scandinavia closer to the rest of Europe. And in a world full of borders, we need more bridges. Recognizing this is vital. At the time of COP26, we were approaching eight billion people[4] sharing one home with 8.7 million species of plants and animals.[5] We had apportioned this home into nearly two hundred entities, which we call countries. Around them, we had built borders, which are seen by our species but by very few others. We build these borders for our protection and to mark out what we call our own. The plants and animals. The land itself. The rocks beneath us.

The seas around us. Even the space occupied by the air above us. We call it our airspace. But the air itself is not our own. It comes and goes, mixing freely with air from other airspaces. It is shared by everyone and everything. All living things depend on it. With the widest of the straits beneath me, I pondered on this simple truth, and I hoped that it would be reflected in any agreement that would be made in Glasgow.

When I changed trains in Cologne on the morning of the second day, I peered upward, and through the curved glass roof of the station, I could see Cologne Cathedral. It is beautiful. The 157-meter-tall Gothic edifice is built of an elegant white sandstone, which is blackened by acid rain. It took over six hundred years to build the cathedral, and I cannot help thinking about the person who laid down its foundation stone in 1248,[6] which was before Stockholm was founded. Could that person have ever imagined the five-aisled basilica in its full splendor and the 1,300 trains arriving and departing at its foot every day? That person was part of building something beautiful for future generations. This is what the COP is for. Its ultimate goal is to lay the foundations of a beautiful future for coming generations. I hoped that this second simple truth would not be forgotten in the fervor of the coming negotiation.

The most amazing part of the rail journey is the 50-kilometer-long Channel Tunnel that links the United Kingdom to Europe. In 1994, Queen Elizabeth II, and the French president opened the tunnel which was first proposed in 1802 to Napoleon. The tunnel follows a gently dipping bed of chalk, which is made of small creatures called plankton that lived when there were dinosaurs on Earth. It reaches 75 meters below the seafloor. This underwater bridge is a symbol of both unity and sadness. Eleven million people are carried by the high-speed trains that go through it every year and bring England and France closer together, but, since 2020, each of them crosses a border that was rebuilt as the first wave of the coronavirus loomed on

Figure 18.1 *Cologne Cathedral seen through the curved glass roof of Cologne Main Station, Germany.*

the horizon. As I ponder the sad loss of a nation in which "mainland Europe" became "Europe," a monitor overhead flickered "The world is looking to you, COP26." The train emerged amid the unparalleled grandeur of St. Pancras Station in good time before I needed to board the night train to Glasgow from Euston Station. In its great hall, I could feel the excitement rising. On billboards all around me were the words "Thank you for travelling by train, COP26." It was symbolic, I know, but I still found it beautiful.

The UK was visibly proud to host COP26, and Glasgow was even prouder. One of its pair of main railway stations, Glasgow Queen Street, had become the gateway to the meeting that was tasked with changing the world. There were electric shuttle buses leaving every few minutes for the meeting venue, which is lovingly known by the locals as "the Armadillo" for reasons that become obvious when you

Figure 18.2 *London Euston Station in November 2021, while COP26 was being held in Glasgow, Scotland.*

see its shape. I boarded one of the shuttle buses and sat crammed together with fifty or so face-masked delegates for the fifteen-minute journey to the Blue Zone. This is the part of the COP which can only be accessed by parties and observers. It is where decisions are made. There is also a Green Zone. It is open to all.

The entrance was made easy to find because it was surrounded by climate activists who had converged on Glasgow from all parts of the UK and beyond to share their hopes and fears. One of them was a priest called Annika. She had walked there from Sweden as a pilgrimage from Vadstena Abbey, which is situated in a small town of the same name on the eastern shore of Vättern, Sweden's second largest lake. The pilgrimage had taken four months.

Police officers stood along the entire length of the road that flanked the venue. Their presence was calming. They kept the entranceway clear with only gentle words. They worked with the activists, not against them. Despite the cold misty rain, an aura of warmth enshrouded the entranceway. Glasgow had good reason to be proud.

Perhaps the biggest challenge of all facing Glasgow was keeping the coronavirus out of the COP. It was only weeks before the arrival of Omicron, but I did not know that at the time. I imagine that an earlier arrival of Omicron would have meant postponing the COP a second time. This would have been a disaster.

At the entrance gate, I showed proof of vaccination, a negative test result, my UNFCCC invitation letter, and my passport before I was allowed to enter the arena. I was then allowed to join the queue of delegates and observers which wound backward and forward first outside between metal barriers and then along a covered walkway toward the Armadillo.

Once inside the Blue Zone, I was met by all kinds of artwork, each competing for a sideways glance from one of the delegates rushing between negotiations. Each one carried with it a voice from the outside world to the heart of the arena. My own eyes were captivated by a globe on which *"people live here"* was written on every country in children's handwriting. Beside it was a makeshift wall along which I read the contrasting reflections of adults and children. Adults hid their fear behind clever plays on words, whereas children spoke their fear with crystal clarity:

This is the biggest crisis humanity has ever faced.

Yes, it is.

The Blue Zone was a chaotic maze of meeting rooms and exhibitions. Outside each meeting room was a list of up-and-coming sessions. Outside one, observers had been queuing for hours to catch a glimpse of the American president. Seating was limited, more so because of social distancing restrictions. Not all of them would be allowed in. I did not join them. Instead, I made a mental note to return later. There would be a session on the latest IPCC report. I hoped that its queue would be equally long. I wanted to believe that there was a place in the arena for science.

I entered the main Exhibition Hall and found myself amid a labyrinth of pavilions. It was endless. Some pavilions were glamorous multi-story constructions. Others were simpler with a speaker platform and a seating area. The tempo was crazy. There was a continuous stream of delegates. They hurried past government spokespersons, boasting proudly about pledges that might be enacted in some undefined future, and NGOs vying with one another to place dissociated fragments of the climate crisis on center stage. It was chaos. All I could see were demountable follies to humanity's failure to comprehend the magnitude of the climate crisis. I left.

Before embarking on the journey to COP26, I had watched an elegantly crafted satire in which a dinosaur entered the negotiations. His name was Frankie. He was an expert on mass extinctions. He likened fossil fuel subsidies to funding meteorites. When I joined the nonexistent queue to listen to reflections on the IPCC report in a half-empty auditorium, my heartfelt desire was for Frankie to enter the arena and explain for everyone why we were there. He did not. So, once again, I left.

My first impressions of the COP were more a reflection of my own naivety. What I failed to see amid the chaos of the arena were the painstaking efforts made by negotiators to break free from a multifaceted system which, even if it is of our own making, locks humanity in.

We need giant steps. But we must acknowledge small steps.

The small step at COP26 concerned fossil fuel subsidies and phasing out coal. The role of the COP President is to move negotiations forward by challenging the status quo and finding consensus. The president's challenge was worded:

> The Conference of the Parties calls upon Parties to accelerate the phasing out of coal and subsidies for fossil fuels.

The watered-down consensus which made it into the Glasgow Climate Pact[7] was worded:

> The Conference of the Parties calls upon Parties to accelerate the development, deployment and dissemination of technologies, and the adoption of policies, to transition towards low-emission energy systems, including by rapidly scaling up the deployment of clean power generation and energy efficiency measures, including accelerating efforts towards the phasedown of unabated coal power and phase-out of inefficient fossil fuel subsidies, while providing targeted support to the poorest and most vulnerable in line with national circumstances and recognizing the need for support towards a just transition.

I was devastated when I read it, but this too reflected my own naivety. Greenpeace, who have been in this game far longer than I have been, wrote as follows:

> For the first time ever, coal power, and fossil fuels subsidies were mentioned in the written agreement. This is a breakthrough.

Two years later, in the Global Stocktake[8] from COP28 in Dubai, this formulation had become:

> Transitioning away from fossil fuels in energy systems, in a just, orderly and equitable manner, accelerating action in this critical decade, so as to achieve net zero by 2050 in keeping with the science.

"Phasedown" had become "transitioning away" and "coal" had become "fossil fuels."

Small steps.

The small step which was taken in Glasgow belongs to everyone who was there and everyone who tried to be there. It belongs to the negotiators in the arena and the activists on its outside. It is owned by the musician who called a ceilidh in the rain outside of the arena uniting negotiators and climate activists in dance. It belongs to the priest who walked there from Vadstena and to the police who watched over us making sure that we were safe. And, most of important of all, it belongs to the people who tried so hard but could not get there because of the coronavirus restrictions or because the visa process was too slow.

In these dark times, I try to acknowledge even the smallest of successes, and I encourage you to do the same. These small steps are brought to fruition by us all. Together. United against the wave.

19

Alternative Futures

Our time is the moment when the wave crests the horizon. In this moment, we still have choices. There are alternative futures. We can stand still and watch as the wave engulfs us all. We can turn our backs on the children who are playing in the sand and run to protect ourselves. Or we can call them away from the shore and run together.

The IPCC call these alternative futures SSPs.[1]

The acronym SSP stands for Shared Socioeconomic Pathway, which is hardly easier to understand than the acronym itself. The shared socioeconomic pathways are stories about alternative futures. There are five of them. They are written by multidisciplinary teams of scholars from just about every discipline.

Each story focuses on aspects of futures that affect greenhouse gas emissions, such as how many people we will be on Earth, whether the economy will carry on growing, how much energy we will use, how much of that energy will come from fossil fuels, if we will live in cities or in the countryside, and how our behavior might change.

Various guesses about future climate policies are then added to each story. The purpose of these policies (using the language of the IPCC) is to limit "radiative forcing." This term can be a little confusing. Radiative forcing refers to the difference between the amount of energy reaching the Earth and its atmosphere from the Sun and the amount of energy radiated from the Earth and its atmosphere back into space. In the context considered here—radiative forcing caused by humans—we find that this difference arises for two reasons. The greenhouse gases we are adding to the atmosphere trap energy that would have otherwise escaped from an atmosphere unaffected by humans. This causes "positive" radiative forcing, making the climate *warmer*. However, humans not only add greenhouse gases to the atmosphere; they also add miniscule particles called aerosols. These particles are added to the atmosphere as a "by-product" when we burn fossil fuels as well as various types of biomass. Certain aerosols reflect sunlight back into space. This causes "negative" radiative forcing, making the climate *cooler*. Importantly, cooling caused by humans adding aerosols to the atmosphere is *far less* than warming caused by humans adding greenhouse gases to the atmosphere. Therefore, reducing radiative forcing caused by humans will limit global warming.

In 2019, radiative forcing caused by humans was 2.72 watts per meter squared.[2] Reducing this number to 1.9 watts per meter squared by 2100 would have the effect of limiting global warming to 1.5 degrees. This can be achieved by massively reducing the amount of greenhouse gases we add to the atmosphere. This is what we promised to do when we signed the Paris Agreement.[3]

A worrying sidenote about radiative forcing caused by humans is that warming caused by greenhouse gases lasts *far longer* than cooling caused by aerosols. For this reason, some of the warming we have caused by adding greenhouse gases to the atmosphere may be temporarily "masked" by cooling caused by the aerosols we added to the atmosphere at the same time. In other words, global warming might actually be worse than it appears to be.

One of the five alternative futures, which the IPCC call SSPs, is called "Middle of the Road." Its basis is that we will do as we always have done. As the climate crisis worsens, we will act as we did when we faced other crises in the past. Our response will be similar to our responses to past wars, economic crises, and pandemics. This story makes sense. It seems logical to assume that we will respond as we always have done. In its sixth assessment report, the IPCC combine this story with climate policies that are not unlike current ones. If this story comes to fruition, which, based on current policies and actions,[4] might well happen, our children will face a future with 2.7 degrees of warming.

Now that we are getting a flavor of what going beyond 1 degree of warming actually means, we can begin to envisage the horror that 2.7 degrees of warming will bring. In this future, heatwaves, which will be more than 2 degrees hotter than the ones we are experiencing currently, will be happening four times more frequently; floods and droughts will be more severe and happening twice as often; sea level will have risen by around half a meter; and one in twenty species will be at risk of extinction.[5]

Another story is called "Taking the Highway." This one is even more scary. In this story, we make sure that the economy keeps growing by carrying on burning fossil fuels. With the climate policies chosen for the example given by the IPCC in its sixth assessment report, we find that this story ends with our children facing more than 4 degrees of warming. They are left with no choice but to try out various kinds of geoengineering in desperate attempts to cool an overheated Earth.

And I am not referring to the safe kind of geoengineering in which carbon dioxide is captured from the air and stored underground. I am referring to very scary and really bad kinds of geoengineering in which we attempt to shield ourselves from the Sun by cloaking the Earth by artificially injecting "mirror-like" aerosols into the upper atmosphere. The idea is that these miniscule chemical particles will reflect sunlight (causing negative radiative forcing) and cool our burning planet. There are numerous reasons why this is a bad idea. First of all, the chemical in question is most likely to be sulfur dioxide. This chemical reacts with other gases in the air to make sulfuric acid which is a corrosive poison. This is a problem because, after a few weeks, the particles will fall out of the sky, contaminating the world below. Then there are all of the unknown effects on weather patterns. Will it rain in the same places? Probably not. We know this from past volcanic eruptions (which also inject particles into the air). If rainfall patterns change, who gets to decide who gets rain and who does not? Then there is the scariest part of all. If we actually managed to cool the Earth by adding chemical particles to the upper atmosphere, we risk creating a false sense of security that would allow us to carry on poisoning the air that we breathe by continuing to burn fossil fuels. And when the inevitable happens and we can no longer continue adding chemical particles to the upper atmosphere (we run out of money, we start fighting with each other—even more than we do now), we enter what scientists call "terminal shock."[6] The carbon dioxide that we had continued to add to the atmosphere would cause the Earth's temperature to skyrocket upward far faster than living things can adapt to. A not unlikely outcome of terminal shock is a sixth mass extinction.

Two of the other stories have similar themes. These are called "A Rocky Road" and "A Road Divided." Both stories are about inequality, either between countries, or within countries. We make futile efforts to protect ourselves with borders. Each country fights for itself. Rich countries or rich people take care of themselves. Poor countries or poor people are left behind. These are the most dystopic of the SSPs. Common to each of them is that climate models predict that we will quite likely fail to curb global warming.[7] This makes sense, because the atmosphere does not care about our borders. These are the stories that end with a few of us as "survivors," standing on the hills far from the shore and looking down on the swirling waters that swallowed the children we left behind.

The fifth story is called "Taking the Green Road." This is the story that is most easily paired with the ambitious climate policies that are needed to bend the curve of climate change.

The IPCC call the most optimistic of these pairings "SSP1-1.9"—where "1.9" refers to limiting radiative forcing to 1.9 watts per meter squared by 2100, that is, what we need to do to keep the promise we made when we signed the Paris Agreement. In this story, we achieve carbon neutrality by 2050. This means that, by that time, our remaining greenhouse gas emissions are balanced by efforts to remove carbon dioxide from the air (naturally and artificially).

In this story, we switch our focus from economic growth to the well-being of humans and nature. We stop mindlessly consuming stuff that we do not need. We focus on equity and care across space and time. We give nature a chance to repair the damage we have caused. And the gift we pass on to our children is that they get to be alive when global warming peaks and starts to wane. And as the Earth cools, our children will experience how heatwaves become less extreme and less frequent, and how the worst floods and droughts happen less often.

This is a story in which we stand witness as the hierarchical duality between humans and nature that Descartes wrote about in his correspondence with Queen Kristina shatters into pieces. And emerging in its place, we find a complex entwinement between ourselves and nature—an entwinement that acknowledges how our futures and the futures of all living things are woven together in a seemingly endless tapestry.

This is a beautiful story in which we call our children away from the shore, and we hold their hands, and we run together.

This beautiful story must be our story.

20

Our Story

We know exactly what we must do. We know exactly how to write our story.

The IPCC have spelled it out for us for more than thirty years.

The solution to the climate crisis has three parts, and we need them all.[1] The first part of the solution is to reduce the greenhouse gas emissions that are causing the climate crisis in the first place. The second part is to get help from nature. And the third part is to find artificial ways of removing carbon dioxide from the air.

The part of the solution we find hardest to act on is reducing greenhouse gas emissions.[2] It raises so many questions. Who should reduce emissions? The rich or the poor? Individuals or governments? What about the remaining carbon budget (whatever that is)? Who gets how much of it?

The Paris Agreement, which almost all of our countries have signed, has a principle that helps us answer some of these questions. It is called the "Principle of Common but Differentiated Responsibilities and Respective Capabilities."[3] Abbreviating it to CBDR&RC doesn't make it any easier to understand. There are two parts to this principle.

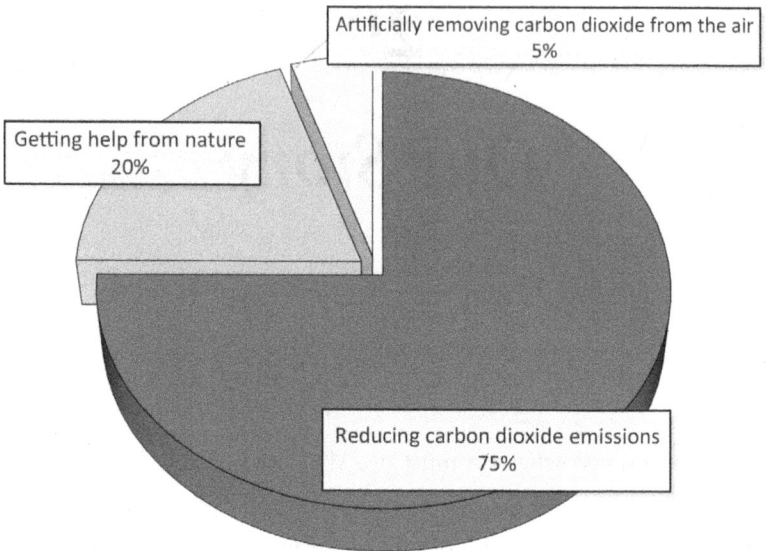

Figure 20.1 *The three parts of the solution to the climate crisis, all of which are needed, all at the same time. Proportions are averages for the five illustrative mitigation pathways (for carbon dioxide) shown in figure SPM.5 of the Working Group III contribution to the Sixth Assessment Report of the IPCC (2022).*

These are responsibility and capability. Responsibility concerns the past. How much of any riches I or my country have acquired was made possible by emitting greenhouse gases in the past? The principle states that I or my country bears some responsibility for these past emissions. Capability concerns fulfillment of basic needs. I or my country must first be able to fulfill our basic needs before we are tasked with reducing greenhouse gas emissions. What these principles boil down to is that richer people and countries need to reduce greenhouse gas emissions faster than poorer people and countries. This means that the remaining carbon budget (a very uncertain number[4] which states how much carbon dioxide we can still emit and nevertheless keep global warming below some temperature that is in line with the Paris Agreement—preferably 1.5 degrees but usually 2 degrees) cannot be divided equally between peoples and countries. Instead, poorer people, and countries must receive the lion's share.

On an individual basis, you are the only person who knows your own status with regard to the principles of responsibility and capability. You are the only person who knows how much you can and should reduce your own emissions, if at all. Individual emission reductions are just that. Individual. It is wise not to judge another person's emissions as you will never know all aspects of their circumstances. This is because capability encompasses far more than material wealth. What if, for health reasons, a person cannot eat less meat? What if a person's family situation makes it impossible to fly less? What if a person cannot afford to take the train or buy an electric car? What if there is no railway? What if a person lives in a colder climate where an electric car does not work because the battery drains too fast? What if a person has a medical condition which makes it impossible to use public transport? These are all real factors which must be considered when deciding on one's capability of reducing greenhouse gas emissions.

If my status is such that I can reduce my greenhouse gas emissions (and mine is), knowing where they come from makes it easier to make meaningful decisions. In this respect, a good starting principle is that every single molecule of carbon dioxide that does not end up in the atmosphere is a success. This is because it takes a very long time for that carbon dioxide molecule (or, to be more precise, one it exchanges with) to return to the rocks where it came from. This means that "only recycling" is not so "only." It is a valid contribution to the solution to the climate crisis. Yet, as individuals, many of us can do far more than "only recycling."

Getting around is a massive source of greenhouse gas emissions. Irrespective of how I transport myself, there will be emissions. But

I can choose ways of getting around which emit less than others. In general, public transport is better than private cars, even if they are electric ones. It is simply more efficient to move a lot of people around in one large vehicle (such as a bus or a train) rather than lots of smaller vehicles (such as cars). Unfortunately, the same is not true for planes. This is because planes use so much fuel that even though a plane carries lots of people, greenhouse emissions per person are higher than for other modes of transport.

There is a fair chance that when I set out to reduce my emissions from traveling, I will encounter difficulties which I cannot overcome myself. For example, I can only use public transport if it exists and if it takes me all the way home. If it doesn't, I might have no other option than to go by car. This is when my government plays in. I need its members to make sure that the public transport network really works. What if I want to travel by train, but I cannot afford it because it costs more than flying? Should it cost more? Should I need to buy tickets from multiple operators for a single rail journey? Perhaps not. Once again, I need my government (and governments of neighboring countries) to make it possible for me to reduce my own emissions. The answer to the question "Individuals or governments?" is "Both."

Then there is one more question that I can ask myself: Is my journey necessary at all? A journey that is not made has no emissions at all. Can I work from home sometimes? But if I do, what happens to the collegiality that makes a workplace function? Can I combine one trip with another one, cutting my emissions by a factor of two? What about longer journeys? Can I go on holiday? Where is the balance between seeing the world so that I care about it and emitting so much that I am party to destroying it? These are difficult questions to answer, and there is no "one-size-fits-all" answer. We are all individuals with very different lives. A first step is acknowledging that there are no easy answers and that it is wise to stop and think before "just doing."

Heating or cooling my home can be another massive source of emissions. This will, of course, depend on where I live and if I can afford to heat or cool my home. Or if I have a home at all. If I have a home and I can afford to heat it or cool it, I might be able to reduce my greenhouse gas emissions by changing where my energy comes from, and regardless of where my energy comes from, I will be able to reduce my emissions by reducing how much energy I use.

The energy we use to keep ourselves warm (or cool) comes from all different sources. It might be from burning fossil fuels or from burning wood or other types of biomass. It might come as electricity, but this too comes from somewhere. Electricity can come from renewable sources, such as solar panels, wind turbines, hydroelectric dams, and wave generators. It can be nuclear. It can come from burning biomass, or fossil fuels. I first need to find out where my energy comes from and if this is pre-decided for me or if I can choose myself. If I can, I can choose wisely. Choosing wisely means choosing renewables. This is because renewable energy is energy harnessed from sources which do not get used up over time, such as sunlight, wind, waves, tidal currents, or flowing rivers. Also, producing renewable energy emits much less carbon dioxide into the air than most other forms of energy production.

Burning fossil fuels is clearly a bad idea. This releases carbon (as carbon dioxide), which has been stored in rocks for hundreds of millions of years, causing it to "pile up" in the air that we breathe, where it strengthens the greenhouse effect, causing global warming, and worsening the climate crisis. But what about burning biomass and nuclear power?

Energy production by biomass burning is sometimes considered to be "carbon neutral." This would imply that the amount of carbon dioxide added to the air by biomass burning is exactly balanced by the amount of carbon dioxide which was removed from the air by whatever we are burning while it was still alive. This would be good if it were true. Sometimes it is, but often it's not. In the context of energy production, biomass means all sorts of things. Biomass can mean wood pellets made from wood left over after production of timber or furniture, or a so-called "black liquor," which is left over after production of pulp and paper. Biomass can also mean wood pellets made from fast-growing trees which were planted specifically for producing biomass for burning. Biomass can be agricultural waste or crops planted specifically for producing biomass for burning. Biomass can be waste from our homes, such as leftover food. Biomass can even be animal manure and our own feces. It matters a lot where biomass comes from. For example, biomass burning, which uses fast-growing trees planted specifically for that purpose, cannot be carbon neutral. This is because when we cut down a tree to burn it, it stops removing carbon dioxide from the air instantly, and even if we plant a new tree straight away, it will take some time before that tree has grown large enough to be able to remove the same amount of carbon dioxide from the air as the tree that was cut down did. This delay means that less carbon dioxide is removed from the air. This has exactly the same effect on the amount of carbon dioxide in the air as adding carbon dioxide to the air by, for example, burning fossil fuels. This means that burning this type of biomass is not carbon neutral. Also, plantations of fast-growing trees are less good at supporting biodiversity and less good at taking up carbon dioxide than natural woodlands, which they often replace. This takes us even further away from carbon neutrality.

Nuclear power seems like a good option from a climate perspective because greenhouse gas emissions from nuclear energy production are very low. But there is a catch. A small amount of the leftovers from nuclear energy production is high-level radioactive waste. This means that it is dangerously radioactive for a very long time. "Very long" from a geological perspective means hundreds of thousands or millions of years, which is, from our perspective, "forever." This is a problem, because to produce nuclear energy responsibly entails finding safe ways of storing high-level nuclear waste for a very long time. In Sweden, where I live, this is especially problematic. This is because the time it takes for some high-level radioactive waste to become safe is so long that we already know now that it will still be highly dangerous during the next glaciation.[5] This is a problem, because during a glaciation, massive ice sheets weigh down on the Earth's surface, and when they finally melt away, the Earth's surface bounces back. This happens quickly at first with lots of earthquakes. Thus, nice stable rocks such as the 1.9-billion-year-old granites which are found in Sweden become unsafe momentarily, which can cause damage to underground storage sites for high-level radioactive waste, causing it to leak out and contaminate the surroundings. Does this matter? It will be one hundred thousand years from now, or perhaps two hundred thousand years from now if our greenhouse gas emissions cause one glacial advance to be missed out. Do we have a responsibility for what happens in one hundred or two hundred thousand years?

I often take my students to a postglacial fault, which runs across a small isle in the Stockholm Archipelago. It is a several-meter-deep fissure filled with fractured pieces of rock. It was formed after the last glaciation, probably by a similar-sized earthquake to the ones that shake Iceland and California today. Peering down into this fissure, I ask my students to ponder on the question of responsibility over hundreds of thousands of years. They do and so do I.

Even if I am at liberty to choose renewables, I am still left with one more question. Can I reduce the amount of energy I use? I mentioned before that since the start of the Great Acceleration, population has risen by a factor of three, while energy consumption has risen by a factor of five. This can only mean one thing. It means that we use more energy per person now than we did in the quite recent past. Do we need to? Are we happier because of it? Even renewable energy production is reliant on resources which come from the Earth and are in short supply. The rare Earth elements are good examples. They are called rare Earth elements because they are rare. Yet they are critical for the production of high-power magnets, which convert wind energy into electricity, and the photovoltaic cells, which do the same with sunlight. They come from minerals found in rocks, which take hundreds of millions of years to form. They must be mined, and those mines need to be somewhere. Perhaps, I can be a part of reducing an overdependence on Earth's finite resources by notching the temperature in my home down by a couple of degrees in the winter and accepting it being a couple of degrees warmer in the summer. These small choices make a difference because I am not alone. I am not only an individual; I am part of a collective. If every person in my country did exactly the same for one year, our collective effort would result in two hundred thousand tons of carbon dioxide not ending up in the air.[6]

What and how much stuff I buy also matters. There are greenhouse gas emissions associated with just about everything I buy. Emissions might arise when a product is being manufactured or when it is transported to the place where I then buy it. Buying stuff is most often a choice. I can choose to buy something or not to buy it. I can stop for a second and ask myself if I really need what I am about to buy. I can even ask myself if I actually want what I am about to buy or if the person I am buying it for actually wants it. Have you ever struggled to find a gift for someone and ended up buying one anyhow even though you know that the item you have just bought is probably one that that person does not really want? But you buy it anyway because it feels wrong to come empty-handed. I have.

I can of course blame advertising for my purchases. An economist I know once told me that the purpose of advertising is to make me feel that I am not beautiful enough or that I am not smart enough or that I am not happy enough, and that if only I buy this one product, I will be smarter, happier, and more beautiful. Should my government regulate advertising? Should it be made clear for me how much the product I am about to buy contributes to making the Earth hotter? Of course, I can choose to ignore advertising and not buy whatever it is anyhow. This is my choice, even if it is sometimes quite hard.

I might be told that buying stuff is good for the economy. It helps it grow bigger. It is so important that it grows that the eighth Sustainability Development Goal (SDG for short) is called "Decent Work and Economic Growth." "Decent Work" makes sense, but why "Economic Growth?" It is as if the economy is some kind of thing that I need to care for. Is it? Yet if I do feed it and it does grow, humans will consume more resources, and resources are finite because the Earth is not becoming any larger. Surely, I have more important things than the economy to care for?

And then there is pricing. Is it fair? Should the prices of the things I buy reflect their true cost by including the cost future generations will be forced to pay in the perilously overheated world that overconsumption will cause?

The food that I eat is another source of greenhouse gas emissions. These emissions are different than emissions from getting around and heating (or cooling) our homes. This is because emissions from food production are not only carbon dioxide but also methane and nitrous oxide. These greenhouse gases are far more potent than carbon dioxide, meaning that they warm the Earth more effectively. On the other hand, there is far less methane and nitrous oxide in the air compared with carbon dioxide, and unlike carbon dioxide, which effectively resides in the air for many thousands of years,[7] methane and nitrous oxide have comparatively short effective residence times in the air. This means that cutting emissions of methane and nitrous oxide will cool the Earth more quickly, but that continuing to emit carbon dioxide will warm the Earth for longer. This faster response makes it tempting to focus on emissions from food production. This makes some sense, but it is still vital to not lose focus on carbon dioxide because our carbon dioxide emissions will continue to affect the climate for hundreds of thousands of years.

When it comes to emissions from food production, regardless of how I choose to count and which studies I choose to refer to, emissions from meat production are higher than emissions from producing vegetables. This means that if my health allows it and if I am in a position that allows me to choose freely what I eat, I can substantially reduce my own greenhouse gas emissions by eating more vegetables and less meat. It is good to eat locally and excellent to eat food that is in season, but I will have the most impact on my own emissions if I focus on cutting down on meat, wherever my food comes from.[8] It is also wise not to spend too much time comparing between different meats and different vegetables, as numbers vary quite a lot between different studies. Cutting down on meat does not necessarily mean becoming vegetarian or vegan (although doing so is very good for the climate). One can find good arguments for eating *some* meat, such as the positive effects of grazing livestock on biodiversity. However, one struggles to find good arguments for eating *lots* of meat. There are, of course, exceptions, which is why we need to respect one another's choices. For example, some parts of the world are not well-suited for vegetable production. There can also be cultural reasons for eating a lot of meat. There can be other reasons too. The bottom line is that when it comes to food, I only know with certainty what is the right choice for me.

Even the buildings we live and work in and the infrastructure we rely on for our everyday lives (such as roads and railways) are sources of greenhouse gas emissions. In addition to energy production, the largest sources of greenhouse gas emissions associated with buildings and infrastructure are from the production of cement and steel.

Cement is part of the paste that holds concrete together. We build buildings of concrete. Cement contains silica, alumina, and lime. Silica can come from sand. Alumina can come from clay. Lime is made by burning limestone. Burning limestone releases carbon dioxide to the air. There are three options for reducing emissions from cement production. We can build buildings with something else. Wood can be a good option. We can capture the carbon dioxide that is released when we burn limestone. This can be done by algae, which consume carbon dioxide by photosynthesis, or carbon dioxide can be captured and stored in geological formations (more on that later). We might even be able to use a different rock than limestone to make cement. The rock we might be able to use is called skarn. Skarns are beautiful. They are usually green in color. They contain a mixture of silica, alumina, and lime, but no carbon dioxide. Silica, alumina, and lime are the main ingredients of cement. Because skarns do not contain any carbon dioxide, making cement from skarns does not release any carbon dioxide to the air.

Steel is used for the construction of just about everything. Steel is made of iron, which comes from iron ore, which is a mixture of iron and oxygen. Making iron from iron ore means convincing iron atoms to let go of oxygen atoms. This is challenging because iron atoms are very fond of oxygen atoms. However, carbon atoms are even more fond of oxygen atoms and will happily steal them from iron atoms. Thus, mixing carbon with iron ore in a furnace produces iron (which is used to make steel) and carbon dioxide which is released to the air. There are three options for reducing emissions from steel production.

We can use something other than steel for construction. Once again, wood can be an option, but only for some kinds of construction. We can capture the carbon dioxide which is released and store it in geological formations (once again, more on that later). We can use something other than carbon to steal oxygen atoms from iron atoms. That something can be hydrogen. In the same way that carbon combines with oxygen to make carbon dioxide, hydrogen combines with oxygen to make water. This is clearly better for the climate. However, neither making nor storing hydrogen is straightforward and unless done carefully, the advantages of using hydrogen to produce steel can be outweighed by the disadvantages. Nevertheless, humans are good at inventing stuff. So, my guess is that hydrogen will play a central role in our story.

The second part of the solution is getting help from nature.[9] This part of the solution can seem easier to accept than emissions reductions because nature-based solutions (as they are often called), or NBS, as nature-based solutions is sometimes abbreviated to, do not seem to involve any personal sacrifices. This might be why nature-based solutions are often favored by governments or used by individuals for offsetting emissions (more on that later).

There are three categories of nature-based solutions, which are encompassed by the rather painful acronym LULUCF, which stands for "Land Use, Land-Use Change and Forestry." The parts of nature which can help us solve the climate crisis and are encompassed by this cumbersome expression are forests, agriculture, and wetlands.

There are various ways that we can work together with forests to build a better future. An obvious one is to plant trees where we once upon a time cut them down. This is called reforestation. It is a good idea from a climate perspective because trees are very good at removing carbon dioxide from the air by photosynthesis. It is also a good idea from a biodiversity perspective, because by replanting trees we might be able to restore habitats that we damaged in the past. This means that reforestation can be a win-win for the climate and for biodiversity. It is important not to confuse reforestation with afforestation. The latter means planting trees where there were no trees before. This might seem like a good idea from a climate perspective, because more carbon dioxide will be removed from the air. However, from a biodiversity perspective, we risk damaging or destroying the habitats of whatever lived in the places we subject to afforestation. Another good way of working together with forests is to protect them. This is particularly important when it comes to natural forests. This is because natural forests are not only trees. The floor of a natural forest is carpeted by all kinds of other plants, each of which also removes carbon dioxide from the air. This is made possible because natural forests consist of lots of different types of trees which are of different ages. This makes for a mottled canopy which allows light to penetrate through and reach the forest floor. This, in turn, permits photosynthesis, which allows plants to grow. Natural forests are not just good for the climate. They are also far more biologically diverse than forest plantations. Once again, we have a win-win for the climate and for biodiversity. A third way of working together with forests is to pursue efforts to avoid forest fires. This can be as simple as not allowing campfires at certain times of year or setting up firebreaks so a fire, once started, cannot spread too far. Forest fires occur naturally, and the disturbance they cause can be good for biodiversity, but in a warming world, forest fires are happening far too often, so efforts to curb them are necessary.

Agriculture has a vital role to play in the solution to the climate crisis. Humans need to farm the land to survive, so we cannot just stop farming, but we can take steps toward making agriculture work for the climate, not against it. One way of doing this is to reduce how much we plow the land. When we do so, soil (which is partly carbon) combines with oxygen to make carbon dioxide, often with some assistance from various living organisms. If we plow less, agricultural land might be able to store more carbon for a longer time. However, a farmer is not always at liberty to plow less. Plowing can be essential for retention of water and nutrients, which plants need to be able to grow. There is a fine balance, and a good farmer knows where this balance lies. Another way of making agriculture work for the climate is use of cover crops. These are plants which are not grown to be harvested but to enrich soil with nutrients which are needed by the crops which are to be grown for harvesting. This can create a win-win situation, because cover crops can reduce the need for artificial fertilizers while, at the same time, removing carbon dioxide from the air by photosynthesis. An exploratory approach is to add biochar to soils. Biochar is made from biomass by pyrolysis. This means that it is heated in the absence of oxygen (so that it doesn't make carbon dioxide). Biochar can be added to soils, making them more fertile. What needs to be better understood is how quickly (if at all) biochar combines with oxygen to make carbon dioxide and also if the effects of adding biochar to soils on biodiversity are positive or negative. Other creative solutions include growing crops (most often vegetables) on a smaller scale at home and in cities. This has benefits beyond the obvious one, which is the food that is produced. Growing vegetables at home makes it easier for humans to identify with where food comes from, which in turn can foster respect for nature and the challenges she faces. Growing vegetables and other crops in cities makes cities greener. This brings city residents closer to nature, fostering the same respect. This is especially important for the vast numbers of city residents who lack the socioeconomic means to be able to simply "get out" in nature.

What is perhaps most important of all concerning agriculture is what we use agricultural land for. A general rule is that if a piece of land is used to grow vegetables or grain, we can feed more people than if we use the same piece of land for meat production. This is, of course, not always the case. Some agricultural land is far better suited for livestock than for growing crops. From a climate perspective, we have a lot to gain from working with the land so that land which is good for growing vegetables or grain is used for growing vegetables or grain, and land which is better suited for livestock is used for livestock. The net result will be less meat production, because a lot of land which is well-suited for growing vegetables and grain is presently used for livestock. This is another win-win. Not only can we feed more people, but growing vegetables, and grain is better for the climate because plants remove carbon dioxide from the air by photosynthesis, whereas livestock, especially cows, add greenhouse gases to the air. This is because methane is a by-product of their digestion. It is emitted mostly by belching (not flatulence).

Wetlands are especially important. They not only provide focal points of biological diversity and protection from flooding, but wetlands are also good for the climate. This is because wetlands are poor in oxygen, and without oxygen, carbon cannot become carbon dioxide, so it stays there. Wetlands can store carbon, keeping it safely away from the air, for long periods of time. Wetlands are our friends. Protecting them and restoring them are among the lowest-hanging fruits of nature-based solutions to the climate crisis.

Had we got started earlier, we would not need there to be a third part of the solution. We would not need to consider artificial ways of removing carbon dioxide from the air. But we didn't. This means that carbon dioxide removal[10] (which is what it is called) or CDR, as it is sometimes abbreviated to, has become a necessary part of the solution to the climate crisis. Like nature-based solutions, carbon dioxide removal is often easier to accept than emissions reductions because it too does not seem to require much in the way of personal sacrifices.

There are two stages of carbon dioxide removal. These are capture and storage. This is where we get the expression carbon capture and storage, or CCS, from. Carbon dioxide can be "captured" in two ways. It can be captured at a point source where it would otherwise have been released into the air (a factory chimney, for example), or it can be captured directly from the air. If we begin with capturing carbon dioxide at a point source, once captured, it needs to be separated from the other stuff it was mixed with. It can then be converted at pressure to a liquid or mixed with water to make carbonic acid and carried away to some place where it can be stored safely. These are energy-consuming processes, so it is vital that the energy used comes from renewable sources; otherwise, one ends up swapping one carbon dioxide molecule for another, which is pointless. Carbon dioxide can also be captured from the air. It is passed through a filter that contains some artificial or natural substance which absorbs carbon dioxide. This filter needs to be heated to release the carbon dioxide again so that it can be reused. This also consumes energy, which needs to be renewable for the process to have any real value. The carbon dioxide, once released, can be converted to a liquid or mixed with water and carried away somewhere to be stored. This brings us to the question of storage, for which there are two main options. Carbon dioxide can be stored as a pressurized liquid in sedimentary rocks, which are rocks made of grains of (for example) sand which have been pressed together. These are often (but not always) the same rocks from which oil and gas were once extracted. They are porous (full of holes), so there is plenty of place to store carbon dioxide and because these rocks are found deep down, pressure is sufficiently high for carbon dioxide to remain as a liquid. As to the question of leakage: The oil and gas that were there before did not leak out for millions of years, so it might be safe to assume that the carbon dioxide we pump down there won't leak out either. Carbon dioxide, provided that it is mixed with water as carbonic acid, can also be stored in volcanic rocks. These rocks are not only porous. They are also reactive. Volcanic rocks react with carbonic acid to make minerals called carbonates. These minerals are literally carbon dioxide turned to stone. There is an elegance to this idea, which, as a geologist, I find pleasing. The carbon dioxide we put in the air came from rocks, and by converting it to carbonate minerals, we complete the cycle, returning the carbon dioxide to the rocks again. There is, of course, a catch. This is scale. The capacity for carbon capture and storage, especially the kind in which carbon dioxide is turned to stone, is miniscule compared with the challenge we are facing. If carbon dioxide removal is to play its part in solving the climate crisis, we need to step up our efforts massively.

There is a take-home message concerning climate change solutions which is all too often forgotten. This is that all three parts of the solution (reducing greenhouse gas emissions, getting help from nature, and finding artificial ways of removing carbon dioxide from the air) are needed. This means that we cannot replace one of them with another. All too often, one listens to policymakers arguing about which solution is best. The answer is that they all are. They are all needed. Had we wanted to pick and choose, we would have needed to have started solving the climate crisis a good many years ago. We didn't. We waited. And now we need all three parts of the solution.

This is why carbon offsetting does not work. Carbon offsetting means replacing one part of the solution to the climate crisis with another. For example, a government might motivate waiting with emissions reductions by establishing a scheme for rewetting wetlands, or an individual might compensate for a flight by paying someone to plant trees somewhere. In both cases, we "swap" emissions reductions for nature-based solutions (rewetting wetlands, planting trees). But this is like spending money that we don't have. The wetlands need to be wetted anyhow. The trees need to be planted anyhow. These nature-based solutions are part of the solution to the climate crisis. So are emissions reductions, but if we offset carbon instead of reducing emissions, our emissions are not reduced, and they need to be. It is that simple.

21

The Oak Tree

When I hold public lectures about the climate crisis, I end with one of two reflections on hope. The first one concerns progress we have already made.

I reflect back on the first time I held a public lecture on climate. It was in 2013, shortly after I was appointed as Director of the Bolin Center for Climate Research. I remember referring to a "business-as-usual" scenario for 2100 with global warming of 4 degrees. This number came from the fifth assessment report of the IPCC, which was published that year.[1]

Four degrees of global warming is quite simply terrifying. In a 4-degree warmer world, we can expect eight times more heatwaves that are up to 4 degrees hotter than the ones we are experiencing today.[2] We can also expect a doubling of the number of floods and droughts (which, combined with heat waves, set the stage for wildfires), many of which will be more severe than the ones we are experiencing today. The sea will have risen by another half meter by 2100, and it will continue to rise for centuries thereafter. Most concerning of all is that the proportion of our emissions taken up by the sea and the land will be halved, meaning that more carbon dioxide will end up in the air and the Earth will get hotter faster than is happening right now.

This will make climate zones move faster too, making it even harder for living things to keep pace. In other words, in a 4-degree warmer world, we will find ourselves spiraling toward a mass extinction.[3]

At the time of writing, current policies, and actions put us on target for 2.7 degrees of warming in 2100.[4]

This is still terrifying, but not as terrifying as 4 degrees.

What this tells us is that a lot has happened in one decade. There was the Paris Agreement, which set the 1.5-degree target, and the Glasgow Climate Pact, which kept it "alive" and which contained the first mention of phasing down coal and fossil fuel subsidies. There is also a massive and sustained rise in public awareness of the climate crisis. This can be tied statistically (based on browser search trends) to Greta Thunberg sitting down in Parliament Square and each of the climate strikes that followed. There are efforts made by a handful of wise politicians, often swimming upstream, in response to pressure from their voters and from businesses in response to pressure from their customers. There is the hard work of millions of individuals from across the entire world, each living ordinary lives, each making first small steps and then larger ones toward a way of life that fits within the planetary boundaries. Each contribution is miniscule compared to the enormity of the climate crisis, and it is easy to feel that it makes no difference, but it does. When added together, millions of small contributions make a far larger one. Together we can and are making a difference.

We are halfway there.

2.7 degrees is halfway from 4 degrees to 1.5 degrees.

My second reflection on hope is about an oak tree.

It is an oak tree on an island that is called Visingsö.

The island is fourteen kilometers long, narrow, and low-lying. It occupies most of the southern end of Vättern, the second largest lake in Sweden, alongside which is Vadstena Abbey, from where Annika led her pilgrimage to COP26. Vättern is 135 kilometer long, and its average width is fourteen kilometers. It fills a massive 800 million year old valley, which creates a natural divide between the once rival kingdoms of West and East Götland. It is magnificent. It is like the sea. Looking westwards from its eastern shore, one might see across to the other side. Looking along its length its sparkling waters merge with the horizon.

Visingsö is ornamented with patchworks of fields and copses in varying shades of green. Legend tells us that Visingsö was made from a piece of turf cast out in the middle of Vättern by a giant called Vist. His purpose was to make a stepping stone so that his sweetheart, who was smaller than he was, could cross the lake in two strides rather than one. Be that as it may, Visingsö is among the most beautiful places I have had the privilege of being.

The crossing from the mainland port in the village of Gränna to Visingsö takes half an hour. On a calm day, if one closes one's eyes, one would not know that one was on a lake at all. Halfway across, one passes the other ferry, returning from the island. Both of them are painted vivid yellow. Fifteen minutes later, the ferry reaches the island port. It is a quick turnaround. The captain uses the engines to keep the ferry up against the pier.

Visingsö is special for geologists and for historians. There are stromatolites on the northern end of the island, which makes it special for geologists, and there is a ruined fortress at its southern end, which makes the island special for historians, for it is from this fortress that the kingdoms that would become Sweden were once ruled.

Not much remains of this fortress. There is a curved wall with one opening beyond which a walkway can be followed above the cliffs, which tower over southern Vättern. The walkway passes around the side of a curved buttress in which there is a low doorway. Through it, one enters a circular chamber, which is contained within the buttress itself. Resting against the sandstone walls, bending forward because of their curvature, I am surrounded by history. I am cast back in time, eight hundred years to when rule over Sweden passed four times between rivaling dynasties. The first one was the family of Sverker the Old. He was from eastern Götland, a kingdom which extends northwards across Svealand and Norway. The other one was the family of Erik the Holy. He was from western Götland, a kingdom which extended southwards across Skåne and Denmark. Each time power passed back and forth between these dynasties, a king would die of fever or of some other mysterious cause, and always between the curving walls of the fortress at the southern end of Visingsö.

Sitting in half darkness, listening to the distant lapping of waves on the shore below, I find myself pondering on the eerie thought that all that separates us from those kings of old is time. We are so close to them, and we are also so faraway. This is the mystery of time. It is both a bridge and a barrier.

As we face the climate crisis and choose how we will respond, we may find it of value to learn from the Aboriginal people of Australia, who see themselves moving backward into the future, facing their ancestors. This is of value because we are forced to ask how they will look back at us. Are we good ancestors?

Between the island port and the ruined fortress are the oak woods, which is where I will end this story.

The oak woods of Visingsö are famous. Most of the trees in the oak woods are not oaks at all. They are beeches. But there are oaks. They are recognizable by the rough appearance of their bark and its coating of a silvery-yellow moss wherever it is reached by sunlight penetrating through the leafy green canopy overhead. The reason that so many beech trees were planted in an oak wood is that beech trees force oak trees to grow straight and tall. This is because beech trees create a canopy, which is hard for sunlight to penetrate. The oak trees must grow straight and tall to reach the light.

The oak trees were planted by order of the Swedish Navy in 1831. This was to ensure the supply of timber for shipbuilding, which is why the oak trees needed to be so tall and straight. They were due to be harvested in 1975, but by then, ships were no longer made of timber. They were made of metal. This is why there are still oak trees on Visingsö.

In summertime, a spiritual silence fills the oak woods. Glimpses of sunlight find small openings in the beech canopy overhead and cast solitary rays onto the carpet of russet brown leaves far below.

Stand with me now with those magnificent oak trees towering above us, and let us cast our minds back in time and picture ourselves planting the seeds from which those great trees would eventually grow.

Would we have known that ships would be built of metal when the oak trees whose seeds we were planting would be full grown?

The future is seldom what we expect it to be.

When we face the climate crisis, and we map it all out ahead of us, and we feel locked in by a system that we see no escape from, and it all becomes too much, and all that we can feel is sorrow for a species that seems so close to the end of its time, we can find guidance in those beautiful oak trees. When facing the future, we have good reason to expect the unexpected, because history teaches us that it is the unexpected that actually happens.

And picturing ourselves once more planting the seeds that would become those oak trees, one thing we would have known for certain

Figure 21.1 *This oak tree was planted on Visingsö, Sweden, in 1831 so that there would be enough oak wood to build ships in the future. It was never harvested.*

is that we would be long gone before they were fully grown. And fully aware of this truth, we would still have planted them. We would not have planted them for ourselves. We would have planted them for generations still to come.

This is what happens when we solve the climate crisis.

This is what happens when we take hold of those whom we hold dearest, when we gather the children from the beach, and when we turn our backs on the wave as it crests the horizon and we run together in search of higher ground.

We do not solve the climate crisis for ourselves. We solve the climate crisis to become good ancestors. And we know we can succeed because our own ancestors planted oak trees for us.

Notes

Prologue

1. IPCC. "Summary for Policymakers." In *Climate Change 2021: The Physical Science Basis. Contribution of Working Group I to the Sixth Assessment Report of the Intergovernmental Panel on Climate Change*, ed. V. Masson-Delmotte, P. Zhai, A. Pirani, et al. (Cambridge: Cambridge University Press, 2021). https://doi.org/10.1017/9781009157896.001

2. Raymo, M. and Ruddiman, W. "Tectonic Forcing of Late Cenozoic Climate." *Nature* 359 (1992): 117–22. https://doi.org/10.1038/359117a0

3. Estimated for 1.2°C of climate warming since 1968 [calculated from: National Oceanic and Atmospheric Administration (NOAA), "Global Times Series." https://www.ncei.noaa.gov/access/monitoring/climate-at-a-glance/global/time-series/globe/land_ocean/ytd/12/1850-2024 (January 25, 2025)] and an average temperature change of 1°C in 3.2 million years for tectonic climate forcing over the past 50 million years [calculated from: Hansen, J., Sato, M., Russell, G., and Kharecha, P. "Climate Sensitivity, Sea Level and Atmospheric Carbon Dioxide." *Philosophical Transactions of the Royal Society* A 371 (2013): 20120294. http://dx.doi.org/10.1098/rsta.2012.0294].

4. Urban, M. C. "Climate Change Extinctions." *Science* 386 (2024): 1123–8. https://www.science.org/doi/10.1126/science.adp4461

5. Song, H., Kemp, D. B., Tian, L. et al. "Thresholds of Temperature Change for Mass Extinctions." *Nature Communications* 12 (2021): 4694. https://doi.org/10.1038/s41467-021-25019-2

6. Mora C., Tittensor, D. P., Adl, S. et al. "How Many Species Are There on Earth and in the Ocean?" *PLoS Biology* 9 (2011): e100112. https://doi.org/10.1038/news.2011.498

Chapter 1

1. Pomonis, A., Rossetto, T., Peiris, N., et al. "The Indian Ocean Tsunami of 26 December 2004: Mission Findings in Sri Lanka and Thailand." Earthquake Engineering Field Investigation Team (EEFIT) Mission Report (2006). https://www.istructe.org/resources/report/eefit-mission-report-india-ocean-tsunami/ (January 25, 2025).

2. Krisinformation.se. "Tsunamin i Sydostasien Annandagen 2004." https://www.krisinformation.se/forbered-dig/handelser-och-storningar/20051/tsunamin-i-sydostasien-annandagen-2004 (January 25, 2025).

3. Mård Karlsson, J., Skelton, A., Sandén, M., et al. "Reconstructions of the Coastal Impact of the 2004 Indian Ocean Tsunami in the Khao Lak Area, Thailand." *Journal of Geophysical Research* 114 (2009): C10023. https://doi.org/10.1029/2009JC005516

4. Lay, T., Kanamori, H., Ammon, C. J., et al. "The Great Sumatra-Andaman Earthquake of 26 December 2004." *Science* 308 (2005): 1127–33. https://www.science.org/doi/10.1126/science.1112250

5. IPCC. "Summary for Policymakers." In *Climate Change 2021: The Physical Science Basis. Contribution of Working Group I to the Sixth Assessment Report of the Intergovernmental Panel on Climate Change*, ed. V. Masson-Delmotte, P. Zhai, A. Pirani, et al. (Cambridge: Cambridge University Press, 2021). https://doi.org/10.1017/9781009157896.001

Chapter 2

1. Welch, B., Coe, D., Diego, J. M. et al. "A Highly Magnified Star at Redshift 6.2." *Nature* 603 (2022): 815–8. https://doi.org/10.1038/s41586-022-04449-y

2. Patterson, C., Tilton, G., and Inghram, M. "Age of the Earth." *Science* 121 (1955): 69–75. https://doi.org/10.1126/science.121.3134.69

3. Kasting, J. F. "Earth's Early Atmosphere." *Science* 259 (1993): 920–6. https://doi.org/10.1126/science.11536547

4. Daly, R. A. "Origin of the Moon and Its Topography." *Proceedings of the American Philosophical Society* 90 (1946): 104–19. https://www.jstor.org/stable/3301051

5   Wilde, S., Valley, J., Peck, W. et al. "Evidence from Detrital Zircons for the Existence of Continental Crust and Oceans on the Earth 4.4 Gyr Ago." *Nature* 409 (2001): 175–8. https://doi.org/10.1038/35051550

6   Catling, C. D. and Zahnle, K. J. "The Archaean Atmosphere." *Science Advances* 6 (2020): 1420. https://doi.org/10.1126/sciadv.aax1420

7   Bell, E. A., Boehnke, P., Harrison, T. M., and Mao, W. L. "Potentially Biogenic Carbon Preserved in a 4.1 Ga Zircon." *Proceedings of the National Academy of Sciences* 112 (2015): 14518–21. https://doi.org/10.1073/pnas.1517557112

8   Walter, M., Buick, R., and Dunlop, J. "Stromatolites 3,400–3,500 Myr Old from the North Pole Area, Western Australia." *Nature* 284 (1980): 443–5. https://doi.org/10.1038/284443a0

9   Lyons, T., Reinhard, C., and Planavsky, N. "The Rise of Oxygen in Earth's Early Ocean and Atmosphere." *Nature* 506 (2014): 307–15. https://doi.org/10.1038/nature13068

10 Mitchell, R. N., Zhang, N., Salminen, J. et al. "The Supercontinent Cycle." *Nature Reviews Earth and Environment* 2 (2021): 358–74. https://doi.org/10.1038/s43017-021-00160-0

11 Cawood, P. A. and Hawkesworth, C. J. "Earth's Middle Age." *Geology* 42 (2014): 503–6. https://doi.org/10.1130/G35402.1

12 Hoffman, P. F., Kaufman, A. J. Halverson, G. P., and Schrag, D. P. "A Neoproterozoic Snowball Earth." *Science* 282 (1998): 1342–6. https://doi.org/10.1126/science.281.5381.1342

13 Harry B. Whittington. *The Burgess Shale* (Newhaven: Yale University Press, 1985).

14 Kenrick, P., Wellman, C. H., Schneider, H. and Edgecombe, G. D. "A Timeline for Territorialization: Consequences for the Carbon Cycle in the Paleozoic." *Philosophical Transactions of the Royal Society B* 367 (2012): 519–36. https://doi.org/10.1098/rstb.2011.0271

15 Schulte, P., Alegret, L., Arenillas, I., et al. "The Chicxulub Asteroid Impact and Mass Extinction at the Cretaceous-Paleogene Boundary." *Science* 327 (2010): 1214–8. https://doi.org/10.1126/science.1177265

16 McInerney, F. A. and Wing, S. L. "The Paleocene-Eocene Thermal Maximum: A Perturbation of Carbon Cycle, Climate, and Biosphere with

Implications for the Future." *Annual Review of Earth and Planetary Sciences* 39 (2011): 489–516. https://doi.org/10.1146/annurev-earth-040610-133431

17 Raymo, M. and Ruddiman, W. "Tectonic Forcing of Late Cenozoic Climate." *Nature* 359 (1992): 117–22. https://doi.org/10.1038/359117a0

18 Hren, M. T., Sheldon, N. D., Grimes, S. T., et al. "Terrestrial Cooling in Northern Europe During the Eocene–Oligocene Transition." *Proceedings of the National Academy of Science* 110 (2013): 7562–7. https://doi.org/10.1073/pnas.1210930110

19 Tattersall, I. "Human Origins: Out of Africa." *Proceedings of the National Academy of Science* 106 (2009): 16018–21. https://doi.org/10.1073/pnas.0903207106

20 Klein Goldewijk, K., Beusen, A., Doelman, J.-, and Stehfest, E. "Anthropogenic Land Use Estimates for the Holocene—HYDE 3.2." *Earth System Science Data* 9 (2017): 927–53. https://doi.org/10.5194/essd-9-927-2017

21 IPCC. "Summary for Policymakers." In *Climate Change 2021: The Physical Science Basis. Contribution of Working Group I to the Sixth Assessment Report of the Intergovernmental Panel on Climate Change*, ed. V. Masson-Delmotte, P. Zhai, A. Pirani, et al. (Cambridge, UK: Cambridge University Press, 2021). https://doi.org/10.1017/9781009157896.001

Chapter 3

1 "Aristotle." *Meteorology, Book II, Part 5*, trans. E. W. Webster (350 BCE). https://classics.mit.edu/Aristotle/meteorology.2.ii.html (January 25, 2025).

2 Ptolemy, C. *Almagest, Book II, Part 12*, trans. J. G. Toomer (London: Great Duckworth & Co. Ltd., 1984).

3 World Meteorological Organization, "Climate." https://wmo.int/topics/climate (January 25, 2025).

4 Forster, P., Storelvmo, T., Armour, K. et al. "The Earth's Energy Budget, Climate Feedbacks, and Climate Sensitivity." In *Climate Change 2021: The Physical Science Basis. Contribution of Working Group I to the Sixth Assessment Report of the Intergovernmental Panel on Climate Change*, ed. V.

Masson-Delmotte, P. Zhai, and A. Pirani (Cambridge: Cambridge University Press, 2021): 923–1054. https://doi.org/10.1017/9781009157896.009

5 NASA, "Cosmic Background Explorer." https://lambda.gsfc.nasa.gov/product/cobe/ (January 25, 2025).

6 Calculated using the Stefan-Boltzmann Law – T [Kelvin] = (Es)$^{1/4}$ – with s = Stefan-Boltzmann constant and E (incoming solar radiation) = 340 Wm^{-2} [Forster, P., Storelvmo, T., Armour, K., et al. "The Earth's Energy Budget, Climate Feedbacks, and Climate Sensitivity." In *Climate Change 2021: The Physical Science Basis. Contribution of Working Group I to the Sixth Assessment Report of the Intergovernmental Panel on Climate Change*, ed. V. Masson-Delmotte, P. Zhai, and A. Pirani (Cambridge: Cambridge University Press, 2021): 923–1054. https://doi.org/10.1017/9781009157896.009].

7 Calculated for an albedo of 0.3 [Forster, P., Storelvmo, T., Armour, K., et al. "The Earth's Energy Budget, Climate Feedbacks, and Climate Sensitivity." In *Climate Change 2021: The Physical Science Basis. Contribution of Working Group I to the Sixth Assessment Report of the Intergovernmental Panel on Climate Change*, ed. V. Masson-Delmotte, P. Zhai, and A. Pirani (Cambridge: Cambridge University Press, 2021): 923–1054. https://doi.org/10.1017/9781009157896.009].

8 Hansen, J., Sato, M., Russell, G., and Kharecha, P. "Climate Sensitivity, Sea Level and Atmospheric Carbon Dioxide." *Philosophical Transactions of the Royal Society* A 371 (2013): 20120294. http://dx.doi.org/10.1098/rsta.2012.0294

Chapter 4

1 Walter, M., Buick, R., and Dunlop, J. "Stromatolites 3,400–3,500 Myr Old from the North Pole Area, Western Australia." *Nature* 284 (1980): 443–5. https://doi.org/10.1038/284443a0

2 Intergovernmental Panel on Climate Change. "History of the IPCC." https://www.ipcc.ch/about/history/ (January 25, 2025).

3 Roberts, J. L. and Treagus, J. E. "The Dalradian Rocks of the Southwest Highlands—Introduction." *Scottish Journal of Geology* 13 (1977): 87–99. https://doi.org/10.1144/sjg1302008

4   Hess, H. H. "History of Ocean Basins." In *Petrologic Studies: A Volume in Honour of A. F. Buddington*, ed. A. E. J., Engel, H. L. James and B. F. Leonard (Boulder: Geological Society of America, 1962). https://doi.org/10.1130/Petrologic.1962.599

5   Skelton, A. "Flux Rates for Water and Carbon During Greenschist Facies Metamorphism." *Geology* 39 (2011): 43–6. https://doi.org/10.1130/G31328.1

6   Keeling, C. D. "The Concentration and Isotopic Abundances of Carbon Dioxide in the Atmosphere." *Tellus* 12 (1960): 200–3. https://doi.org/10.1111/j.2153-3490.1960.tb01300.x

7   Pales, J. C. and Keeling, C. D. "The Concentration of Atmospheric Carbon Dioxide in Hawaii." *Journal of Geophysical Research* 70 (1965): 6053–6. https://doi.org/10.1029/JZ070i024p06053

8   Suess, H. E. "Radiocarbon Concentration in Modern Wood." *Science* 122 (1955): 415–7. https://doi-org.ezp.sub.su.se/10.1126/science.122.3166.415.b

9   IPCC. "Policymakers Summary." In *Climate Change: The IPCC Scientific Assessment. Contribution of Working Group I to the First Assessment Report of the Intergovernmental Panel on Climate Change*, ed. J. T. Houghton, G. G. Jenkins, G. G. and J. J. Ephraums (Cambridge: Cambridge University Press, 1990). https://www.ipcc.ch/report/ar1/wg1/

10 Sagan, C. and Mullen, G. "Earth and Mars: Evolution of Atmospheres and Surface Temperatures." *Science* 177 (1972): 52–6. https://doi-org.ezp.sub.su.se/10.1126/science.177.4043.52

Chapter 5

1   Berner, R. A., Lasaga, A. C., and Garrels R. M. "The Carbonate-silicate Geochemical Cycle and Its Effect on Atmospheric Carbon Dioxide Over the Past 100 Million Years." *American Journal of Science* 283 (1983): 641–83. https://doi.org/10.2475/ajs.283.7.641

2   Canadell, J. G., Monteiro, P. M. S., Costa, M. H. et al. "Global Carbon and Other Biogeochemical Cycles and Feedbacks." In *Climate Change 2021: The Physical Science Basis. Contribution of Working Group I to the Sixth Assessment Report of the Intergovernmental Panel on Climate Change*, ed. V. Masson-Delmotte, P. Zhai, and A. Pirani (Cambridge: Cambridge University Press, 2021): 673–816. https://doi.org/10.1017/9781009157896.007

Chapter 6

1. Thomson, J. "On the Stratified Rocks of Islay." *Report of the 41st Meeting of the British Association for the Advancement of Science* (London: John Murray, 1871).

2. Evans, D. A. D. "Stratigraphic, Geochronological, and Paleomagnetic Constraints Upon the Neoproterozoic Climatic Paradox." *American Journal of Science* 300 (2000): 347–433. https://doi.org/10.2475/ajs.300.5.347

3. Budyko, M. I. "The Effect of Solar Radiation Variations on the Climate of the Earth." *Tellus* 21 (1969): 611–9. https://doi.org/10.3402/tellusa.v21i5.10109

4. United Nations Framework Convention on Climate Change. "The Paris Agreement." 2016. https://unfccc.int/process-and-meetings/the-paris-agreement (January 25, 2025).

5. Adamnán of Iona (c. 624–704). "Life of Saint Columba." *University College Cork: Corpus of Electronic Texts*. https://celt.ucc.ie/published/T201040/ (January 25, 2025).

6. Spencer, A. "Late Pre-Cambrian Glaciation in Scotland." *Geological Society, London, Memoirs* 6 (1971): 99. https://doi.org/10.1144/gsl.mem.1971.006.01.02

7. Hoffman, P. F., Kaufman, A. J., Halverson, G. P., and Schrag, D. P. "A Neoproterozoic Snowball Earth." *Science* 281 (1998): 1342–6. https://doi.org/10.1126/science.281.5381.1342

Chapter 7

1. Hansen, J., Sato, M., Russell, G., and Kharecha, P. "Climate Sensitivity, Sea Level and Atmospheric Carbon Dioxide." *Philosophical Transactions of the Royal Society* A 371 (2013): 20120294. http://dx.doi.org/10.1098/rsta.2012.0294

2. McInerney, F. A. and Wing, S. L. "The Paleocene-Eocene Thermal Maximum: A Perturbation of Carbon Cycle, Climate, and Biosphere with Implications for the Future." *Annual Review of Earth and Planetary Sciences* 39 (2011): 489–516. https://doi.org/10.1146/annurev-earth-040610-133431

3 Archer, D., Eby, M., Brovkin, V., et al., "Atmospheric Lifetime of Fossil Fuel Carbon Dioxide." *Annual Reviews of Earth and Planetary Sciences* 37 (2009): 117–34: https://doi.org/10.1146/annurev.earth.031208.100206

4 Heilmann-Clausen, C., Nielsen, O. B., and Gersner, F. "Lithostratigraphy and Depositional Environments in the Upper Paleocene and Eocene of Denmark." *Bulletin of the Geological Society of Denmark* 33 (1985): 287–323.

5 Ryding, S., Klaassen, M., Tattersall, G. J., et al. "Shape-shifting: Changing Animal Morphologies as a Response to Climate Warming." *Trends in Ecology & Evolution* 36 (2021): P1036–48. https://doi.org/10.1016/j.tree.2021.07.006

6 Suess, H. E. "Radiocarbon Concentration in Modern Wood." *Science* 122 (1955): 415–7. https://doi-org.ezp.sub.su.se/10.1126/science.122.3166.415.b

7 Stokke, E. W., Jones, M. T., Riber, L., et al. "Rapid and Sustained Environmental Responses to Global Warming: The Paleocene–Eocene Thermal Maximum in the Eastern North Sea." *Climate of the Past* 17 (2021): 1989–2013. https://doi.org/10.5194/cp-17-1989-2021

8 Barnosky, A., Matzke, N., Tomiya, S. et al. "Has the Earth's Sixth Mass Extinction Already Arrived?" *Nature* 471 (2011): 51–7. https://doi.org/10.1038/nature09678

Chapter 8

1 Milankovitch, M. *Théorie mathématique des phénomènes thermiques produits par la radiation solaire* (Paris: Gauthier-Villars, 1920).

2 Hoffman, P. E. and Schrag, D. P. "The Snowball Earth Hypothesis: Testing the Limits of Global Change." *Terra Nova* 14 (2002): 129–55. https://doi.org/10.1046/j.1365-3121.2002.00408.x

3 Ikeda, T. and Tajika, E. "A Study of the Energy Balance Climate Model with CO2-dependent Outgoing Radiation: Implication for the Glaciation During the Cenozoic." *Geophysical Research Letters* 26 (1999): 349–52. https://doi.org/10.1029/1998GL900298

4 Raymo, M. and Ruddiman, W. "Tectonic Forcing of Late Cenozoic Climate." *Nature* 359 (1992): 117–22. https://doi.org/10.1038/359117a0

5 Song, H., Kemp, D. -B., Tian, L. et al. "Thresholds of Temperature Change for Mass Extinctions." *Nature Communications* 12 (2021): 4694. https://doi.org/10.1038/s41467-021-25019-2

6   Estimated for 1.2°C of climate warming since 1968 [calculated from: National Oceanic and Atmospheric Administration (NOAA), "Global Times Series." https://www.ncei.noaa.gov/access/monitoring/climate-at-a-glance/global/time-series/globe/land_ocean/ytd/12/1850-2024 (January 25, 2025)] and average warming of 1°C in 1000 years at the end of last glaciation [calculated from: Osman, M. B., Tierney, J. E., Zhu, J. et al. "Globally Resolved Surface Temperatures since the Last Glacial Maximum." *Nature* 599 (2021): 239–44. https://doi.org/10.1038/s41586-021-03984-4].

7   IPCC. "Policymakers Summary." In *Climate Change: The IPCC Scientific Assessment. Contribution of Working Group I to the First Assessment Report of the Intergovernmental Panel on Climate Change*, ed. J. T. Houghton, G. G. Jenkins, and J. J. Ephraums (Cambridge: Cambridge University Press, 1990). https://www.ipcc.ch/report/ar1/wg1/ (January 25, 2025).

8   Mora C., Tittensor, D. P., Adl, S. et al. "How Many Species Are There on Earth and in the Ocean?" *PLoS Biology* 9 (2011): e100112. https://doi.org/10.1038/news.2011.498

9   IPBES. "Summary for Policymakers." In *Global Assessment Report on Biodiversity and Ecosystem Services of the Intergovernmental Science-Policy Platform on Biodiversity and Ecosystem Services*, ed. S. Díaz, J. Settele, E. S. Brondízio et al. (IPBES Secretariat, 2019). https://doi.org/10.5281/zenodo.3553579

10 Osman, M. B., Tierney, J. E., Zhu, J. et al. "Globally Resolved Surface Temperatures since the Last Glacial Maximum." *Nature* 599 (2021): 239–44. https://doi.org/10.1038/s41586-021-03984-4

11 Song, H., Kemp, D. B., Tian, L. et al. "Thresholds of Temperature Change for Mass Extinctions." *Nature Communications* 12 (2021): 4694. https://doi.org/10.1038/s41467-021-25019-2

Chapter 9

1   Wanner, H., Pfister, C., and Neukom, R., "The Variable European Little Ice Age." *Quaternary Science Reviews* 287 (2022): 107531. https://doi.org/10.1016/j.quascirev.2022.107531

2   Descartes, R. "To Brégy, 15.i.1650." In *Selected Correspondence of Descartes*, trans. Jonathan Bennett (2017). https://www.earlymoderntexts.com/authors/descartes (January 25, 2025).

3 Descartes, R. "To Chanut, 1.ii.1647." In *Selected Correspondence of Descartes*, trans. Jonathan Bennett (2017). https://www.earlymoderntexts.com/authors/descartes (January 25, 2025).

Chapter 10

1 Calculated for four return flights between Stockholm and Edinburgh and one return journey between Edinburgh and Stirling by petrol car, using "Ecopassenger." https://ecopassenger.org/ (January 25, 2025).

2 Lan, X., Tans, P., and Thoning, K. W. "Trends in Globally-averaged CO_2 Determined from NOAA Global Monitoring Laboratory Measurements." Version Monday, 06-Jan-2025 10:06:16 MST. https://doi.org/10.15138/9N0H-ZH07 (January 25, 2025).

3 Steffen, W., Richardson, K., Rockström, J., et al., "Planetary Boundaries: Guiding Human Development on a Changing Planet." *Science* 347 (2015): 1259855. https://doi.org/10.1126/science.1259855

4 IPCC. "Summary for Policymakers." In *Climate Change 2021: The Physical Science Basis. Contribution of Working Group I to the Sixth Assessment Report of the Intergovernmental Panel on Climate Change*, ed. V. Masson-Delmotte, P. Zhai, A. Pirani et al. (Cambridge: Cambridge University Press, 2021). https://doi.org/10.1017/9781009157896.001

5 James Boswell, *The Journal of a Tour to the Hebrides with Samuel Johnson, LL.D* (London: Cadell and Davies, 1812).

6 R. Weston, "Observations on Alabaster or Gypsum as a Manure." In *Repertory of Arts, Manufactures and Agriculture* (London: Nichols and Sons Printers, 1804).

7 Filippelli, G. M. "The Global Phosphorus Cycle." *Reviews in Mineralogy and Geochemistry* 48 (2002): 391–425. https://doi.org/10.2138/rmg.2002.48.10

8 Gruber, N. and Galloway, J. "An Earth-system Perspective of the Global Nitrogen Cycle." *Nature* 451 (2008): 293–6. https://doi.org/10.1038/nature06592

9 Gulev, S. K., Thorne, P. W., Ahn, J. et al., "Changing State of the Climate System." In *Climate Change 2021: The Physical Science Basis. Contribution of Working Group I to the Sixth Assessment Report of the Intergovernmental Panel on Climate Change*, ed. V. Masson-Delmotte, P. Zhai, and A. Pirani

(Cambridge: Cambridge University Press, 2021): 287–422. https://doi.org/10.1017/9781009157896.004

10 Arrhenius, S. "On the Influence of Carbonic Acid in the Air Upon the Temperature of the Ground." *Philosophical Magazine and Journal of Science* 41 (1896): 237–76.

11 Crutzen, P. "Geology of Mankind." *Nature* 415 (2002): 23. https://doi.org/10.1038/415023a

12 Steffen, W., Broadgate, W., Deutsch, L., et al. "The Trajectory of the Anthropocene: The Great Acceleration." *The Anthropocene Review* 2 (2015): 81–98. https://doi.org/10.1177/2053019614564785

13 Lan, X., Tans, P., and Thoning, K. W. "Trends in Globally-averaged CO_2 Determined from NOAA Global Monitoring Laboratory Measurements." Version Monday, 06-Jan-2025 10:06:16 MST. https://doi.org/10.15138/9N0H-ZH07 (January 25, 2025).

Chapter 11

1 Ritchie, H. "Which Form of Transport Has the Smallest Carbon Footprint?" https://ourworldindata.org/travel-carbon-footprint (January 25, 2025).

2 Calculated assuming that evidence of twenty-eight glacial episodes from the Port Askaig Formation [Ali, D. O., Spencer, A. M., Fairchild, I. F. et al., "Indicators of Relative Completeness of the Glacial Record of the Port Askaig Formation, Garvellach Islands, Scotland." *Precambrian Research* 319 (2018): 65–78. https://doi.org/10.1016/j.precamres.2017.12.005] on Islay and the Garvellachs reflects precession-like forcing of 23 000 years during Snowball Earth meltdown [Skelton, A., Löwhagen, L., Fairchild, I. F. et al. "Stable Isotopes of Oxygen and Hydrogen in Meteoric Water During the Cryogenian Period." *Precambrian Research* 320 (2019): 253–60. https://doi.org/10.1016/j.precamres.2018.11.006].

3 IPCC. "Summary for Policymakers." In *Climate Change 2021: The Physical Science Basis. Contribution of Working Group I to the Sixth Assessment Report of the Intergovernmental Panel on Climate Change*, ed. V. Masson-Delmotte, P. Zhai, A. Pirani et al. (Cambridge: Cambridge University Press, 2021). https://doi.org/10.1017/9781009157896.001

4 Folkhälsomyndigheten. "Bekräftade Fall av Covid-19 i Sverige." https://www.folkhalsomyndigheten.se/faktablad/fall-covid-19/ (January 25, 2025).

5. World Health Organization. "WHO Director-General's Opening Remarks at the Media Briefing on COVID-19 - 11 March 2020." https://www.who.int/director-general/speeches/detail/who-director-general-s-opening-remarks-at-the-media-briefing-on-covid-19---11-march-2020 (January 25, 2025).

6. World Health Organization. "China's Latest SARS Outbreak Has been Contained, but Biosafety Concerns Remain – Update 7." https://www.who.int/emergencies/disease-outbreak-news/item/2004_05_18a-en (January 25, 2025).

7. World Health Organization. "WHO COVID-19 Dashboard." https://data.who.int/dashboards/covid19/ (January 25, 2025).

8. Hanna Ritchie. "Global Inequalities in CO2 Emissions." https://ourworldindata.org/inequality-co2 (January 25, 2025).

9. Pörtner, H.-O., Roberts, D. C., Poloczanska, E. S. et al. (eds), "Summary for Policymakers." In *Climate Change 2022: Impacts, Adaptation, and Vulnerability. Contribution of Working Group II to the Sixth Assessment Report of the Intergovernmental Panel on Climate Change*, ed. H.-O. Pörtner, D.C. Roberts, M. Tignor et al. (Cambridge: Cambridge University Press): 3–33. https://doi.org/10.1017/9781009325844.001

10. Friedlingstein, P., O'Sullivan, M., Jones, M. W., et al. "Global Carbon Budget 2020." *Earth System Science Data* 12 (2020): 3269–340. https://doi.org/10.5194/essd-12-3269-2020

11. Canadell, J. G., Monteiro, P. M. S., Costa, M. H. et al., "Global Carbon and Other Biogeochemical Cycles and Feedbacks." In *Climate Change 2021: The Physical Science Basis. Contribution of Working Group I to the Sixth Assessment Report of the Intergovernmental Panel on Climate Change*, ed. V. Masson-Delmotte, P. Zhai, P., and A. Pirani (Cambridge: Cambridge University Press): 673–816. https://doi.org/10.1017/9781009157896.007

12. Calculated for 36.3 billion tons of carbon dioxide (equivalent to 9.9 billion tons of carbon) with a volume of 556 m^3 for each 1 ton of carbon dioxide and an area of 510 trillion m^2 for the Earth's surface.

Chapter 12

1. Hansen, J., Sato, M., Russell, G., and Kharecha, P. "Climate Sensitivity, Sea Level and Atmospheric Carbon Dioxide." *Philosophical Transactions of the Royal Society* A 371 (2013): 20120294. http://dx.doi.org/10.1098/rsta.2012.0294

2 IPCC. "Summary for Policymakers." In *Climate Change 2021: The Physical Science Basis. Contribution of Working Group I to the Sixth Assessment Report of the Intergovernmental Panel on Climate Change*, ed. V. Masson-Delmotte, P. Zhai, A. Pirani et al. (Cambridge: Cambridge University Press): 3–32. https://doi.org/10.1017/9781009157896.001

3 IPCC. "History of the IPCC." https://www.ipcc.ch/about/history/ (January 25, 2025).

Chapter 13

1 IPCC. "Summary for Policymakers." in *Climate Change 2021: The Physical Science Basis. Contribution of Working Group I to the Sixth Assessment Report of the Intergovernmental Panel on Climate Change*, eds. V. Masson-Delmotte, P. Zhai, A. Pirani et al. (Cambridge: Cambridge University Press): 3–32. https://doi.org/10.1017/9781009157896.001

2 USGS. "M 9.1 – 2004 Sumatra – Andaman Islands Earthquake." https://earthquake.usgs.gov/earthquakes/eventpage/official20041226005853450_30/impact (January 25, 2024)

3 Arrhenius, S. "On the Influence of Carbonic Acid in the Air Upon the Temperature of the Ground." *Philosophical Magazine and Journal of Science* 41 (1896): 237–76.

4 Lay, T., Kanamori, H., Ammon, C. J., et al. "The Great Sumatra-Andaman Earthquake of December 2004." *Science* 308 (2005): 1127–33.

5 National Oceanic and Atmospheric Administration. "WMO Climate Normals." https://www.ncei.noaa.gov/products/wmo-climate-normals (January 25, 2025).

6 Office for National Statistics and US Health Security Agency. "Excess Mortality During Heat-periods: 1 June to 31 August 2022." https://www.ons.gov.uk/peoplepopulationandcommunity/birthsdeathsandmarriages/deaths/articles/excessmortalityduringheatperiods/englandandwales1juneto31august2022 (January 25, 2025).

7 Zachariah, M. Vautard, R., and Schumacher, D. L. "Without Human-caused Climate Change, Temperatures of 40°c in the UK Would Have Been Extremely Unlikely." *World Weather Attribution*. https://www.worldweatherattribution.org/without-human-caused-climate-change-temperatures-of-40c-in-the-uk-would-have-been-extremely-unlikely/ (January 25, 2025).

Chapter 14

1. IPCC. "Summary for Policymakers." in *Climate Change 2021: The Physical Science Basis. Contribution of Working Group I to the Sixth Assessment Report of the Intergovernmental Panel on Climate Change*, eds. V. Masson-Delmotte, P. Zhai, A. Pirani et al. (Cambridge: Cambridge University Press): 3–32. https://doi.org/10.1017/9781009157896.001

2. Otto, F. E. L., Zachariah, M., Saeed, F., et al. "Climate Change Likely Increased Extreme Monsoon Rainfall, Flooding Highly Vulnerable Communities in Pakistan." *Environmental Research: Climate* 2 (2023): 025001. http://doi.org/10.1088/2752-5295/acbfd5

3. Kimutai, J., Barnes, C., Zachariah, M., et al. "Human-induced Climate Change Increased Drought Severity in Horn of Africa." *World Weather Attribution* (2023). https://doi.org/10.25561/103482

4. Ritchie, H. "Global Inequalities in CO2 Emissions." https://ourworldindata.org/inequality-co2 (January 25, 2025).

5. World Weather Attribution. https://www.worldweatherattribution.org/ (January 25, 2025).

6. United Nations Environment Programme. "Spreading Like Wildfire – The Rising Threat of Extraordinary Landscape Fires." *A UNEP Rapid Response Assessment* (2022). https://www.unep.org/resources/report/spreading-wildfire-rising-threat-extraordinary-landscape-fires (January 25, 2025).

7. Kew, S. F., Philip, S. Y., and van Oldenborgh, G. F. "The Exceptional Summer Heat Wave in Southern Europe 2017." in *Explaining Extreme Events of 2017 from a Climate Perspective*, ed. S. C. Herring, N. Christidis, A. Hoell, et al., *Bulletin of the American Meteorological Society* 100 (2019): S49–53. https://doi.org/10.1175/BAMS-ExplainingExtremeEvents2017.1

8. Zachariah, M., Philip, S., Pinto, I. et al. "Extreme Heat in North America, Europe and China in July 2023 Made Much More Likely by Climate Change." *World Weather Attribution* (2023). https://doi.org/10.25561/105549

9. World Weather Attribution. "Climate Change Increased the Likelihood of Wildfire Disaster in Highly Exposed Los Angeles Area." https://www.worldweatherattribution.org/climate-change-increased-the-likelihood-of-wildfire-disaster-in-highly-exposed-los-angeles-area/ (January 28, 2025).

Chapter 15

1. IPCC. "Summary for Policymakers." In *Climate Change 2021: The Physical Science Basis. Contribution of Working Group I to the Sixth Assessment Report of the Intergovernmental Panel on Climate Change*, ed. V. Masson-Delmotte, P. Zhai, A. Pirani et al. (Cambridge: Cambridge University Press): 3–32. https://doi.org/10.1017/9781009157896.001

2. Wilkes, M. A., Carrivick, J. L., Castella, E. et al. "Glacier Retreat Reorganizes River Habitats Leaving Refugia for Alpine Invertebrate Biodiversity Poorly Protected." *Nature Ecology and Evolution* 7 (2023): 841–51. https://doi.org/10.1038/s41559-023-02061-5

3. IPCC. "Summary for Policymakers." In *Climate Change 2021: The Physical Science Basis. Contribution of Working Group I to the Sixth Assessment Report of the Intergovernmental Panel on Climate Change*, eds. V. Masson-Delmotte, P. Zhai, A. Pirani et al. (Cambridge: Cambridge University Press): 3–32. https://doi.org/10.1017/9781009157896.001

4. Ritchie, H. "Global Inequalities in CO2 Emissions." https://ourworldindata.org/inequality-co2 (January 25, 2025).

5. Celsius, A. "Anmärkning om vatnets förminskande så i Östersiön som Vesterhafvet." *Kongliga Swenska Wetenskaps Academiens Handlingar* 4 (1743): 33–50.

6. Lyell C. "I. The Bakerian Lecture. —On the Proofs of a Gradual Rising of the Land Certain Parts of Sweden." *Philosophical Transactions of the Royal Society* 125 (1835): 1–38. http://doi.org/10.1098/rstl.1835.0002

7. Hutton J. "Theory of the Earth; or an Investigation of the Laws Observable in the Composition, Dissolution, and Restoration of Land Upon the Globe." *Transactions of the Royal Society of Edinburgh* 1 (1788): 209–304. https://doi.org/10.1017/S0080456800029227

8. Agassiz, L. "Discours prononcé a l'ouverture des séances de la Société Helvétique des sciences naturelles, a Neuchatel le 24 Juillet 1837." *Actes de la Société Helvétique des Sciences Naturelles* 22 (1837) V–XXXII.

9. Jamieson, T. F. "On the History of the Last Geological Changes in Scotland." *Quarterly Journal of the Geological Society of London* 21 (1865): 161–203.

10. De Geer, G. "Om Skandinaviens nivåförändringar under Kvartärperioden." *Geologiska Föreningens i Stockholm Förhandlingar* 10 (1888): 36–379; 12 (1890): 61–110.

11 Lantmäteriet, "Landhöjning," https://www.lantmateriet.se/sv/geodata/gps-geodesi-och-swepos/Referenssystem/Landhojning/ (25 Jan. 2025).

12 Lantmäteriet. "Landhöjning." https://www.lantmateriet.se/sv/geodata/gps-geodesi-och-swepos/Referenssystem/Landhojning/ (January 25, 2025).

13 Hieronymus, M. and Kalén, O. "Sea-level Rise Projections for Sweden based on the New IPCC Special Report: The Ocean and Cryosphere in a Changing Climate." *Ambio* 49 (2020): 1587–600. https://doi.org/10.1007/s13280-019-01313-8

14 Calculated based on a Linear Extrapolation of Normal "Start of Winter" Data for 1961–1990 and 1991–2020 Using Data from: Swedish Meteorological and Hydrological Institute. "Normal Start för Vintern." https://www.smhi.se/data/meteorologi/kartor/normal/arstid-start/vinter (25 Jan. 2025).

15 Sveriges Meteorologiska och Hydrologiska Institut (SMHI). "Vinter." https://www.smhi.se/kunskapsbanken/meteorologi/arstider/vinter/vinter-1.22843 (January 25, 2025).

16 Sveriges Meteorologiska och Hydrologiska Institut (SMHI). "Månads-, årstids- och årskartor." https://www.smhi.se/data/meteorologi/kartor/normal/arstid-start/vinter (January 25, 2025).

17 Calculated by linear extrapolation from a change to the normal start of winter for the periods 1961–1990 and 1991–2020 of 15–20 days [Sveriges Meteorologiska och Hydrologiska Institut (SMHI). "Månads-, Årstids- och årskartor." https://www.smhi.se/data/meteorologi/kartor/normal/arstid-start/vinter (January 25, 2025)].

18 Loarie, S., Duffy, P., Hamilton, H. et al. "The Velocity of Climate Change." *Nature* 462 (2009): 1052–5. https://doi.org/10.1038/nature08649

19 Barnosky, A., Matzke, N., Tomiya, S. et al. "Has the Earth's Sixth Mass Extinction Already Arrived?" *Nature* 471 (2011): 51–7. https://doi.org/10.1038/nature09678

Chapter 16

1 Whitmarsh, R. B., Beslier, M.-O., Wallace, P. J. et al. *Proceedings of the Ocean Drilling Program, Initial Reports 173* (College Station, Texas: Ocean Drilling Program, 1998). http://dx.doi.org/10.2973/odp.proc.ir.173.1998

2 Whitmarsh, R., Manatschal, G., and Minshull, T. "Evolution of Magma-poor Continental Margins From Rifting to Seafloor Spreading." *Nature* 413 (2001): 150–4. https://doi.org/10.1038/35093085

3 Woodland Trust. "Hobby." https://www.woodlandtrust.org.uk/trees-woods-and-wildlife/animals/birds/hobby/ (January 25, 2025).

4 Sweetlove, L. "Number of Species on Earth Tagged at 8.7 Million." *Nature* (2011). https://doi.org/10.1038/news.2011.498

Chapter 17

1 Gogina, M., Zettler, M. L., Wåhlström, I. et al. "A Combination of Species Distribution and Ocean-biogeochemical Models Suggests That Climate Change Overrides Eutrophication as the Driver of Future Distributions of a Key Benthic Crustacean in the Estuarine Ecosystem of the Baltic Sea." *ICES Journal of Marine Science* 77 (2020): 2089–105. https://doi.org/10.1093/icesjms/fsaa107

2 *The Guardian*. "School Climate Strikes: 1.4 Million People Took Part, Say Campaigners." https://www.theguardian.com/environment/2019/mar/19/school-climate-strikes-more-than-1-million-took-part-say-campaigners-greta-thunberg (January 25, 2025).

3 *Vox*. "How Big Was the Global Climate Strike? 4 Million People, Activists Estimate." https://www.vox.com/energy-and-environment/2019/9/20/20876143/climate-strike-2019-september-20-crowd-estimate (January 25, 2025).

Chapter 18

1 United Nations Framework Convention on Climate Change. "Conference of the Parties (COP)." https://unfccc.int/process/bodies/supreme-bodies/conference-of-the-parties-cop (January 25, 2025).

2 Lan, X., Tans, P., and Thoning, K. W. "Trends in Globally-averaged CO_2 Determined from NOAA Global Monitoring Laboratory Measurements." Version Monday, 06-Jan-2025 10:06:16 MST. https://doi.org/10.15138/9N0H-ZH07 (January 25, 2025).

3   IPCC. "Summary for Policymakers." In *Global Warming of 1.5°C. An IPCC Special Report on the Impacts of Global Warming of 1.5°C above Pre-industrial Levels and Related Global Greenhouse Gas Emission Pathways, in the Context of Strengthening the Global Response to the Threat of Climate Change, Sustainable Development, and Efforts to Eradicate Poverty*, ed. V. Masson-Delmotte, P. Zhai, and H.-O. Pörtner (Cambridge: Cambridge University Press, 2018). https://doi.org/10.1017/9781009157940.001

4   Ritchie, H., Rodés-Guirao, L., Mathieu, E. et al. "Population Growth." https://ourworldindata.org/population-growth (January 25, 2025).

5   Sweetlove, L. "Number of Species on Earth Tagged at 8.7 Million." *Nature* (2011). https://doi.org/10.1038/news.2011.498

6   World Heritage Convention (UNESCO). "Cologne Cathedral." https://whc.unesco.org/en/list/292/ (January 25, 2025).

7   United Nations Framework Convention on Climate Change. "Glasgow Climate Pact." https://unfccc.int/documents/310475 (January 25, 2025).

8   United Nations Framework Convention on Climate Change. "Outcome of the First Global Stocktake." https://unfccc.int/sites/default/files/resource/cma2023_L17_adv.pdf (January 25, 2025).

Chapter 19

1   O'Neill, B. C., Kriegler, E., Ebi, K. L. et al. "The Roads Ahead: Narratives for Shared Socioeconomic Pathways Describing World Futures in the 21st Century." *Global Environmental Change* 42 (2017): 169–80. https://doi.org/10.1016/j.gloenvcha.2015.01.004

2   IPCC. "Summary for Policymakers." In *Climate Change 2021: The Physical Science Basis. Contribution of Working Group I to the Sixth Assessment Report of the Intergovernmental Panel on Climate Change*, ed. V. Masson-Delmotte, P. Zhai, A. Pirani et al. (Cambridge: Cambridge University Press): 3–32. https://doi.org/10.1017/9781009157896.001

3   United Nations Framework Convention on Climate Change. "The Paris Agreement." 2016. https://unfccc.int/process-and-meetings/the-paris-agreement (January 25, 2025).

4   Climate Action Tracker. https://climateactiontracker.org/ (January 25, 2025).

5 Urban, M. C. "Climate Change Extinctions." *Science* 386 (2024): 1123–8. https://www.science.org/doi/10.1126/science.adp4461

6 Trisos, C.H., Amatulli, G., Gurevitch, J. et al. "Potentially Dangerous Consequences for Biodiversity of Solar Geoengineering Implementation and Termination." *Nature Ecology and Evolution* 2 (2018): 475–82. https://doi.org/10.1038/s41559-017-0431-0

7 Rogelj, J., Popp, A., Calvin, K. V. et al. "Scenarios Towards Limiting Global Mean Temperature Increase below 1.5 °C." *Nature Climate Change* 8 (2018): 325–32. https://doi.org/10.1038/s41558-018-0091-3

Chapter 20

1 Shukla, P. R., Skea, J., Reisinger, A. et al. (eds.), "Summary for Policymakers." In *Climate Change 2022: Mitigation of Climate Change. Contribution of Working Group III to the Sixth Assessment Report of the Intergovernmental Panel on Climate Change*, ed. P. R. Shukla, J. Skea, R. Slade et al. (Cambridge: Cambridge University Press, 2022). https://doi.org/10.1017/9781009157926.001

2 Ritchie, H. "Sector by Sector: Where Do Global Greenhouse Gas Emissions Come from?" https://ourworldindata.org/ghg-emissions-by-sector (January 25, 2025).

3 United Nations Framework Convention on Climate Change. "The Paris Agreement." https://unfccc.int/process-and-meetings/the-paris-agreement (January 25, 2025).

4 Lamboll, R. D., Nicholls, Z. R. J., Smith, C. J., et al. "Assessing the Size and Uncertainty of Remaining Carbon Budgets." *Nature Climate Change* 13 (2023): 1360–7. https://doi.org/10.1038/s41558-023-01848-5

5 International Atomic Energy Agency. *Classification of Radioactive Waste, IAEA Safety Standards Series No. GSG-1* (IAEA: Vienna, 2020).

6 Calculated for an average area for living per person of 42 sq. m. for Sweden and for a 2 °C lowering of indoor temperature in the winter months and allowing a 2 °C higher indoor temperature in the summer months. Data from Statistics Sweden, https://www.scb.se/en/ (January 25, 2025).

7 The effective residence time for carbon dioxide added by humans to the atmosphere refers here to the time taken for its total amount in the

atmosphere to fall back to pre-industrial levels. This will take many thousands of years [Archer, D., Eby, M., Brovkin, V. et al. "Atmospheric Lifetime of Fossil Fuel Carbon Dioxide." *Annual Reviews of Earth and Planetary Sciences* 37 (2009): 117–34. https://doi.org/10.1146/annurev.earth .031208.100206]. Individual carbon dioxide molecules in the air can swap with other ones in (e.g.) plants, but this only affects which carbon dioxide molecules are in the atmosphere, not how many of them there are.

8   Poore, J. and Nemecek, T. "Reducing Food's Environmental Impacts through Producers and Consumers." *Science* 360 (2018): 987–92. https://www.science.org/doi/10.1126/science.aaq0216

9   Griscom, B. W., Adams, J., Ellis, P. W. et al., "Natural Climate Solutions." *Proceedings of the National Academy of Science* 114 (2017): 11645–50. https://doi.org/10.1073/pnas.1710465114

10 Anderson, K., Buck, H.J., Fuhr, L. et al., "Controversies of Carbon Dioxide Removal." *Nature Reviews Earth and Environment* 4 (2023): 808–14. https://doi.org/10.1038/s43017-023-00493-y

Chapter 21

1   IPCC. "Summary for Policymakers." In *Climate Change 2013: The Physical Science Basis. Contribution of Working Group I to the Fifth Assessment Report of the Intergovernmental Panel on Climate Change*, ed. T. F. Stocker, D. Qin, G.-K. Plattner et al. (Cambridge: Cambridge University Press): 3–30.

2   IPCC. "Summary for Policymakers." in *Climate Change 2021: The Physical Science Basis. Contribution of Working Group I to the Sixth Assessment Report of the Intergovernmental Panel on Climate Change*, ed. V. Masson-Delmotte, P. Zhai, A. Pirani et al. (Cambridge: Cambridge University Press): 3–32. https://doi.org/10.1017/9781009157896.001

3   Urban, M. C. "Climate Change Extinctions." *Science* 386 (2024): 1123–8. https://www.science.org/doi/10.1126/science.adp4461

4   Climate Action Tracker. https://climateactiontracker.org/ (January 25, 2025).

Index

adaptation. *See* climate change adaptation
advertising   157
aerosol masking   144–5
aerosols   144
afforestation   161
Agassiz, Louis   114
Agricultural Revolution   15–16, 22, 76–8
agricultural solutions   161–3
albedo effect   19
   Ice Age   60–1
   Snowball Earth   44
Antarctic Ice Sheet   111
Anthropocene   79
anthropocentricism   61
Arctic sea ice loss   111
Aristotle   17–18
Arrhenius, Svante   79

biochar   162
biodiversity loss
   melting ice   111–12
   migratory birds   123–4
   moving climate zones   118–20
   Paleocene-Eocene Thermal Maximum   56–7
   speed of warming   62
biodiversity
   wildfires   106

biomass burning. *See under* energy
blackbody   19
Boring Billion   13

Cairngorms (Scotland)   33–6
carbon (dioxide)
   budget   150–1
   capture and storage   164–5
   geological cycle   38
   neutrality   147
   offsetting   165–6
   removal   163–5
   roots of mountains   27–8
care between generations   88, 171–3
CBDR&RC. *See* Common but Differentiated Responsibilities and Respective Capabilities
CCS. *See* carbon capture and storage
CDR. *See* carbon dioxide removal
Celsius, Andrius   113
cement   159
chemical weathering. *See* weathering
civil disobedience   124–5
climate
   activism   133–4
   adaptation (*see* climate change solutions)
   energy balance   19–20
   definitions   17–19
   feedbacks (*see* feedbacks)

(in)justice 87, 105
movement 91
normals 99
mitigation (see climate change solutions)
stable states 59
strikes 128–31
zones 118–20
climate change solutions 149
climate crisis
  metaphor x–xiii, 1–6, 81–2
  relating to 64–5, 72–3, 89
  roots 70–1
Climate Live 92
coal. See fossil fuels
Cologne Cathedral (Germany) 136
Common but Differentiated Responsibilities and Respective Capabilities 149–51
Conference of the Parties 134–5
consumption. See under reducing emissions
continental drift 93
COP26 137–42
COP. See Conference of the Parties
coronavirus
  fall in emissions 87
  pandemic 85–6
  vaccination 87
cover crops 162
cows 163
Crutzen, Paul 79

De Geer, Gerald 114
Descartes, René
  correspondence with Queen Kristina 67–70
  death of 71–2
  God 70
  love 69–70
  monument 71
  Stockholm 68–9

droughts 104

economic growth 157
emissions reductions. See reducing emissions
energy
  biomass 153–4
  fossil fuels 153
  burning of 97, 104
  nuclear power 154–5
  reduced use of 155–6
  renewables 153
eutrophication 78

faint Sun paradox 30–1
feedbacks
  negative 106
  positive 106, 112
flooding 104
forests 160–1
Fridays for Future 128
Fur (Denmark) 52–7

gas, natural gas. See fossil fuels
geoengineering 146
geological time
  metaphor 8–16
glaciation
  definition 59
  last glaciation (evidence of) 63
  next glaciation (averting/stalling of) 61–2
Glasgow (Scotland) 137–42
global warming (speed of)
  compared with last glaciation (end of) 61–2, 65
  compared with PETM hyperthermal (onset of) 52
  compared with Snowball Earth (end of) 84–5

government responsibility. *See under* responsibility
Great Acceleration   79
Great Oxygenation Event   12
greenhouse
  effect   20
  gases (*see* carbon dioxide; methane; nitrous oxide)
  state   59
Greenland Ice Sheet   111

heat waves
  Great Britain (July 18–19, 2022)   98–100
  man-made   97
  Sweden (January 1, 2023)   100–1
Hess, Harry   26
High Coast (Sweden)   114–15
Highland Clearances   76
Himalaya
  global cooling   15
Hinba. *See* Holy Isle (Scotland)
Hobby falcon   124
Holocene   61
Holy Isle (Scotland)   43–9
Homo Sapiens
  emergence   15
  taxonomy   21
hope
  metaphor   171–3
  progress   168
  and youth   96, 131–2
Hutton, James   113–14
hydrogen   160
hyperthermal
  definition   14
  evolutionary adaptations 55–7
  global warming (comparison with)   57
  PETM   52

Ice Age
  causes   60–1
  definition   59
  Theory   114
icehouse state   59
individual responsibility. *See under* responsibility
Industrial Revolution   78
intergenerational care. *See* care between generations
interglacial   59
Intergovernmental Panel on Climate Change
  establishment   23
  first assessment report   28–9, 62
  objectives   94
IPCC. *See* Intergovernmental Panel on Climate Change
Islay (Scotland)   23–7, 29–30, 41, 80–1, 83–4

Jamieson, Thomas   114

Keeling curve   28
Keeling, Dave (Charles)   28
Kristina. *See* Queen Kristina

land rise
  evidence   113
  High Coast   114–15
  and sea level rise   115–16
  Stockholm   115–16
  theories   113–14
Land Use, Land-Use Change and Forestry   160
Little Ice Age   68
LULUCF. *See* Land Use, Land-Use Change and Forestry
Lyell, Charles   113

MAPA. *See* Most Affected People and Areas
mass extinction
  and climate change 58
  fifth 14
  sixth xii, 62, 65, 119–20, 146
Mauna Loa 27–8
mayflies 112
methane 157–8
Milanković cycles 59
mitigation. *See* climate change solutions
Most Affected People and Areas 94–5
mountain glaciers 112

natural climate solutions. *See* nature-based solutions
nature-based solutions 160–3
nature-culture dualism 70
NBS. *See* nature-based solutions
nitrogen 77–8
nitrous oxide 157–8
nuclear energy. *See under* energy
Nuna 12

ocean circulation (weakening of) 111
Ocean Drilling Program 121–4
oil. *See* fossil fuels

Paleocene–Eocene Thermal Maximum. *See* hyperthermal
Pangea
  and climate 52
  definition 14
Paris Agreement 42, 134
PETM. *See* hyperthermal
phosphorus 76–7
photosynthesis 12
planetary boundaries 75

plate tectonics 26
plowing 162
polar bears 111
postglacial rebound. *See* land rise
pricing 157
Ptolemy 17

Queen Kristina (of Sweden)
  correspondence with René Descartes 67–70
  life 67

radiative forcing
  by aerosols 144
  definition 143–5
  by greenhouse gases 144
rail journeys 130, 135–7
raised beaches. *See* raised shorelines
raised shorelines 114–15
rare earth elements 156
reducing emissions
  cement 159
  consumption (buying stuff) 156–7
  food 157–8
  heating or cooling our homes 153–6
  steel 159–60
  travel (getting around) 151–2
reforestation 161
renewable energy. *See under* energy
Researchers' Desk 129
responsibility
  governments 152
  individuals 151, 152
Rodinia 13
Runrig 75–6, 81–2

sea level rise
  causes 112
  climate justice 112

and land rise   115–16
Stockholm   115–16
seafloor spreading   26
seasons (fading of)   35–6
shape shifting   56–7
shared socioeconomic pathways
   definition   143
   descriptions   145–8
silicate weathering. *See* weathering
skiing   33–4
Snowball Earth
   causes   13
   end of   48
   Holy Isle   43–8
   Islay   41–2, 80–1, 84–5
   tipping point   41, 44
SSP. *See* shared socioeconomic
   pathways
steel   159–60
Stockholm (Sweden)   62–4, 113, 115–18
stromatolite   11–12, 21–2
subduction   38
Suess effect   28
Suess, Hans   28
sunlight   19

terminal shock   146
Thunberg, Greta   91, 128, 130
tipping points
   PETM hyperthermal   58
   Snowball Earth   42

uncertainty   103–4

Visingsö (Sweden)   168–71
volcanism
   and climate   38, 93
   PETM hyperthermal (cause of)   52
   Snowball Earth (end of)   48

weather attribution
   definition   105
   droughts (Africa)   104
   floods (Pakistan)   104
   heatwaves (UK)   100
   wildfires (Portugal)   107
weathering
   and climate   36–8, 93
   Ice Age (cause of)   60
   PETM hyperthermal (end of)   52
   Snowball Earth (cause of)   44
wetlands   163
wildfires
   biodiversity   106
   California (2025)   109
   causes   106
   Europe (2023)   108
   Portugal (2017)   107–8
winter (end of)   117–18

young activists   92, 94–5, 127–32

About the Author

Alasdair Skelton was born at Loch Ness, Scotland, in 1968. Married with two daughters, he lives in Stockholm, Sweden. He is professor of geochemistry and petrology at Stockholm University. He has published over seventy academic papers on geology, earthquakes, tsunamis, and climate change. He was director of the Bolin Centre for Climate Research for nine years. He is a passionate educator and public speaker. He co-founded Researcher's Desk, a non-profit organization that bridges between academia and civil society and pursues knowledge-based solutions to the climate crisis. As a climate activist, he has supported the youth who created the climate movement that must change the world. In his lifetime, he has witnessed climate change that would have taken four million years to occur naturally.